Copyright © 1979 by Publications International, Ltd.
All rights reserved
Printed in the United States of America

Published by
Harper & Row, Publishers
10 East 53rd Street
New York, New York 10022

Library of Congress Catalog Card Number: 78-20157
ISBN: 0-06-010854-1

Decorating Your Office For Success

**By the editors of Consumer Guide®
with John Pile, consultant for
office design and planning**

HARPER & ROW, PUBLISHERS

NEW YORK

Cambridge
Hagerstown
Philadelphia
San Francisco

1817

London
Mexico City
Sao Paulo
Sydney

Contents

Credits

K. S. Wilshire, Inc., Cover Photo

Brock Arms & Associates, pages 71 bottom, 74 top, 78 bottom, 79 bottom

Associated Space Design, page 80 top

B. Brukoff Interiors, pages 65, 69 top, 72 top

Norman DeHaan & Associates, pages 67 bottom, 77 top, 80 bottom

Jeanne Hartnett & Associates, pages 72 bottom, 74 bottom

Herry Interiors, page 77 bottom

Holabird & Root, page 76

Interior Environments, page 69 bottom

ISD, Inc., pages 73, 78 top

Perkins & Will, page 68 top and bottom

K. S. Wilshire, Inc., pages 66, 67 top, 70, 71 top, 75 top and bottom, 79 top

Foreword: A Setting For Success

Your office can be one of the most effective tools of your work or profession. If you use it to its full potential, it will work to your advantage and support your career. However, if you ignore its potential, it will almost surely work against you.

An office that is a setting for successful work does not develop by chance. It takes knowledgeable thought and planning to create an office space that will benefit you.

Many people continue to hold to the notion that an office is merely a kind of workshop. It seldom is. Although due attention must be given to the utilitarian aspects of your office, it is important also to consider your office in a larger context, too. But first, let us examine the qualities of an office that promote efficient work.

Your Office as a Successful Work Place

To a degree, every office could be considered a workshop. It is a place where materials, tools and equipment are kept and work is carried on with them. Also, the office is a center of visual, verbal and written communication between the occupant and the people he deals with.

You need not be a specialist in "human engineering" or

"human factors research" to understand the basics of making an office an effective functional unit. Tools, materials and equipment should be located in order of diminishing importance. That which you need to have readily at hand—writing materials, phone, reference sources, often-used files—should be closest to you. Everything else in the office should be located as close to you as its frequency of use warrants. Other basic considerations are work surfaces whose size, shape and height match the work processes, and a comfortable chair that provides freedom of movement and that is psychologically suited to the user. An office also should offer adequate lighting that is easy on the eyes, a degree of protection from noise, and whatever level of privacy you need. Distracting clutter should be avoided, but certain kinds of clutter that serve as stimulation must be accommodated. These standards seem very simple, yet a high percentage of offices—including very elaborate and luxurious ones—violate them.

Complying with the standards of convenience and comfort benefits visitors as well as yourself. Because a visitor's exposure to the office is brief, you may think that he does not notice substandard efficiency and comfort. But you have to consider that the visitor is not accustomed to the particular office situation and is therefore likely to be more sensitive to problems and shortcomings. You may be accustomed to a glaring light, an uncomfortable chair, surrounding noise or a clutter of paperwork. But to a visitor, these can be quite unsettling. Any of these may lead the visitor to believe that the office is not adequate to fulfill the need for which he came to it. And that is a reflection on your own adequacy.

Making your office satisfactory in terms of these practical issues is not an overwhelming, difficult matter. You just need to think carefully about what normal work processes are (or should be) carried on in the office, and then seek out appropriate arrangements to support these processes with a minimum of confusion and waste. The reason so many offices are unsatisfactory is that they are hastily thrown together, rather than planned. Most people believe that a desk, a chair or two, file cabinets and ceiling lights will serve any office purpose, even when their placement is haphazard. A factory, laboratory, or even a car put together in this fashion would be a useless monstrosity. Because the office functions are so much easier to provide for, we tend to dismiss the importance of providing even the most reasonable and minimal practical necessities.

Your Office Expresses Your Qualities

Although we may not often think about it, we all take for granted that the way we talk, dress and act express our individual style and personality. Your office is the home base for your career, and, even if you use it only part of the time, you must realize that it also expresses your style and personality. People size you up by the appearance of your office as easily as by the other clues you give to your character.

Visitors will assume that your office is the way it is because you want it that way. Although this assumption may be only partially accurate, it will still be made. It does not matter that you have no control over the office's location, size or furnishings. The visitor will still assume that it is exactly to your liking, and he will use its condition to form an impression of your personality and style.

Of course, in the long run, other aspects of your working style are more important than the image projected by your office. Given time, your real abilities and qualities (your problems and limitations, too) will probably outweigh anything that your office alone may express. Many situations, however, do not offer the time for people to know you through your actions, and even over a long period of time, an office that projects a bad impression will become a burden to you.

The audience that will react to the image your office expresses will naturally depend on the nature of your career and, in part, on your geographic location. But there is always an audience, and it is certain to be influenced, even if the nature of the influence is vague. Basically, there are three types of audience: yourself, outside visitors, and co-workers.

You are the Primary Audience

You are the one person who is *certain* to be influenced by your office, even if you do not realize it. Each time you enter your office—perhaps dozens of times each day—you respond emotionally, even if you don't notice how you are affected. Coming into your office should lift your spirits, not depress you. If you are bored or depressed by mess or confusion, or reminded of how your work limits your abilities or ambitions, something is wrong. Your office is working against you. The sight of your office should suggest interesting and exciting things about to happen, and remind

you of the best-loved parts of your work. It should encourage you to work on what needs to be done. And it should relay the message that the person who works there is creative, exciting, interesting and enjoyable. Your office should give you this kind of psychological and emotional support. Even if no other person *ever* enters your office, it should do this for you.

Outside Visitors

Clients, customers, consultants and peers from outside your organization form the next audience of importance. The best way to consider the reactions of the outside visitor is to think about how you have felt when visiting other peoples' offices. We have all visited someone's office at one time or another, and in every case we have developed a distinct impression.

Some companies choose
for their employees an
open-office layout, which,
though often very attrac-
tive, tends to maximize
function and minimize
personal expression.
Shown is the Action
Office open plan
system from Herman
Miller, Inc.

You can expect your visitors to react to a strange office in the same way as you do. Particularly on a first visit, before the development of an impression by other means, the visitor will tend to size you up on the basis of your setting. They will do it in stages, beginning with your neighborhood, and following a string of impressions from your building, entrance, lobby, and reception area to your office. Take a good look at your office. Is it what one might expect from the preliminary impressions? Is it a pleasant surprise or a discouraging letdown? If you were not in the office and a visitor arrived, would it give him an accurate impression of you?

For your office to serve you to its fullest, it must project accurate, favorable information. If the information is accurate and unfavorable, you have problems that office design cannot overcome. It is a rare occurrence, but sometimes an office can impart an inaccurate but favorable image of you. To aim for this kind of inaccuracy which suggests that things are better than they really are, is an allowable "white lie" in the business world. In fact, an office that expresses character, creativity, skill and achievement that are a touch beyond the facts may even help to improve the realities to match the image.

Using a completely objective approach, you should decide for yourself whether or not your office projects an accurate, favorable image. You cannot depend upon the comments of visitors. The rules of etiquette and common decency cut us off from information about what visitors' impressions may be. A guest cannot say "How can you stand working in this miserable dump?" without being a boor. It is never safe to trust the perfunctory "What a nice office" either, because it is all too likely to have no more meaning than a polite pleasantry like, "You're looking great."

Co-workers

Your co-workers—peers, junior employees, secretaries, assistants and superiors—are inside visitors. These people have an opportunity to learn about you through direct communication, and they have a better basis for understanding what aspects of your office are out of your control. They know what is standard and cannot be altered. They also have more frequent and extended exposure to your office. So, they can sort out what is truly *you* and what is merely the norm of the situation in which you all exist.

Having this inside information, co-workers are most

likely to judge your compatibility with the organization by the "true" signals they receive from your office. They will be looking to see if you are a reasonable person, well suited for the organization—in control of your destiny, but managing that destiny within a context that the organization suggests. If your space is a perfect carbon copy of every other office in the organization, you could be judged to be an anonymous cog in a machine. On the other hand, if it is so different that it looks odd, it could suggest that you are a misfit, unrelated to the realities of your organization.

Fortunately, the same standards that are involved in making your office right for yourself and outside visitors will almost certainly be effective in making it right for this internal audience.

Individuality Vs Stereotype

Think of your office in terms of a "set" for a play. You are the character in the play, and the "set" should visually suggest the type of environment in which you would most logically be found. This is important, because before people know how you think and act, they will react to you in terms of expectations that your "set" projects.

Inevitably, people who come to your office will bring with them preconceptions based on stereotype formulas. If your office is large and comfortable, with ample windows affording a good view from the high floor of a major building, they will presume that you are a person of importance and influence. Dark paneling and graceful antiques will spark the assumption that you are somewhat conservative and that you relate to others in a reserved, conventional way. A dark, dingy office in a state of confusion tells the visitor that you are probably an ineffective cog in a bureaucratic machine. If your office is neat and trim, and identical to all the others in its row, it will hint that you are an "organization man," effective in your role, but totally interchangeable with anyone else in the organization.

These assumptions may, of course, be quite incorrect, but the very fact that people will make them is a factor that you cannot afford to ignore. Set designers for stage, film and TV know and use these stereotype assumptions effectively, and so should you.

In moving toward an office that truly fits your needs, you will inevitably confront a variety of formula solutions to planning problems. Your present office almost surely makes use of some formulas, although they may be outmoded ones. Since millions of offices exist, and the range of office use is quite limited, it is natural to assume that a few designs will take care of most needs. We are, after all, content with a quite small variety of automobiles, and even houses and apartments tend to use a few fairly standard plans. In theory, there would be nothing wrong with a formula office if the formula was truly suited to your practical and psychological needs. In practice, though, the formula tends to make you adapt to the office, rather than having the office serve you. At the same time, the formulas that are abroad in our world are realities to which people have become conditioned.

Formula office design attempts to provide a ready-made visual image that matches some set of intentions. It also tries to offer you a ready-made character that you can put on as easily as you can dress in a business suit. Consistency and repetition, however, reveal artificiality, and mislead people about your style. A furnished hotel suite can be comfortable and even luxurious, but it always remains a hotel suite, an impersonal "set" that has almost no relationship to its occupants. The formula office tends to have these same qualities. Worse yet, it suggests that you may be a formula person—never a promising indication.

You must realize that your own "set" will be evaluated according to certain stereotype formula expectations that are part of the norms of our society. But you must avoid simply accepting any one formula. Instead, find the office that is uniquely right for you.

No one is certain why people react differently to pinks and beiges combined with soft, fuzzy textures than they do to slick, hard surfaces in grays and metallic colors. These communications are obvious even to people who never stop to think about them. The reactions are natural, just as the reactions people experience about you when you are "just being yourself." When you communicate personally with someone, you do not usually plan your actions to make the person understand the real you. But if you expect people to know you through the image your office projects, pre-planning is in order.

Office Status

Organizations, such as the military, which have clearly defined, graded positions for individuals, dramatize status through titles, uniforms, privileges and quarters. This practice has been taken up by highly organized bureaucratic organizations in business. Status orientation tends to focus office planning on a struggle for visible marks of status. Two windows are always better than one, marble tables generally outrank standard wood tables, and both marble and wood outrank metal. The thickness of the carpet is directly related to status level.

Even a brief discussion of the status drive in office design makes most of us recognize its absurdity. The notion that displaying status-identified symbols will in itself create elevated status is as illogical as believing that wearing expensive clothing will make the wearer rich. Status orientation can trap a person, in that it can result in a person placing himself in a well-defined niche within the organization. Also, although the status seeker is always thinking about how high his status is, he usually does not realize that the symbols also make clear how *low* his status may be.

In organizations where status expression is not an enforced policy, status identification has such vague meaning that it can have only incidental effectiveness in any case. An attempt to project an exaggerated status level may not be effective, and even may backfire—resulting in envy and recognition of false pretenses.

The office that works well and expresses your real in-

tentions will naturally contain status symbols to protect you from being undervalued. The best offices do not lead to much thought about status level. They simply communicate "rightness" in other terms that have more substance, and therefore more credibility.

What About Good Taste?

Russell Lynes, in his 1949 book, *The Tastemakers,* generated considerable interest and amusement with charts that classified levels of taste. He called his classifications "Highbrow," "Middlebrow" and "Lowbrow." Unfortunately, games of this sort are not very helpful when planning an effective office environment.

To a great extent, taste, and especially "good" taste, is another form of stereotype formula. Particular groups of people—related by trade, profession, education, age, etc.—often develop a particular "taste" that gives the group identity and cohesiveness. The "taste" of each group may be entirely different, but any claim that one is "good" or better than another is hard to substantiate.

Modern office life is moving away from the snobberies of class distinctions and "old boy" relationships that "tasteful" interior decoration tends to express. In this book we are much more concerned with values that will make your office an ideal place for you to work, and that will express the real you and your real intentions. If these goals are achieved, you can feel confident that the resulting "taste level" will be quite satisfactory.

Function Vs Personal Expression

It is possible for the two key roles of your office, function and personal expression, to come into conflict. For example, your work may require that you surround yourself with a great mass of untidy reference materials, but you may want to show yourself as organized and purposeful. In practice, such conflicts are rare and usually easily resolved. There is often some kind of natural harmony between the image you want to express and the work situation you need. If success in your work requires you to project a methodical and organized image, you should *become* organized and methodical. So, a setting that allows you to work in that way will naturally suggest those qualities in a visual way.

If your aim is to express that you are easy to talk to, arrange your office for convenient conversation. Deal with the

Carefully chosen furniture and accessories can immediately give a visitor to an office the desired impression of the person who works there. Shown are a desk, modular back cabinet, and Posture/Swivel chair from Baker Furniture Co., Contract Division.

practical problems of where people will sit or stand, how they will face and what they will see. In this way, you will find that you give your office space a character that will express what you are aiming for psychologically.

As a rule of thumb, dealing with the problem in the physical sense will automatically produce the desired psychological effect. Exceptions to this rule can arise, however, and need some special thought to resolve. Suppose, for example, that your role in relation to your visitors is quite formal and restrained, but your work requires mounds of paperwork and other materials that are impossible to keep neat and orderly. If you provide the large and formal desk that will hold visitors at a distance and support your style of formality, the clutter on it will make you out to be a disorganized bumbler. In this case, following our rule of thumb will work against you. However, by using your imagination, you could come up with a workable idea as an alternative. Perhaps you could provide two areas, each with its own role. There might be a work area to one side—an area that is not so prominent that it emphasizes the creative clutter of your work. The other area could be more formal, for meetings and conversations, and treated as a focal point of the office. It is almost always possible to find a way to bring your practical and expressive intentions into harmony. It just takes some careful thought.

Evaluating Your Office

The first step in improving your own office is to evaluate your present office situation and your present needs. Then use your conclusions as a basis for planning what should be done. You must also analyze your character, intentions and goals, and think about what image projections are possible within the context of the type of office you use.

On evaluating your office, you will probably find that it falls into one of these four categories:
1. The place has a distinct character, but it is the wrong character and is working against you.
2. It works well in a practical way, but it is institutional and lacks character.
3. The office works well and has a character that expresses your style and personality as it really is.
4. It works well and expresses where you want to be, rather than where you are; it is actively directing you toward success by "speaking" about you to others.

If your office falls into categories one or two, you

should plan to bring it up to the standards required for category three. Reaching category four may take only slight and subtle changes, but you must be careful not to "over-reach." An example of overreaching would be if by some fluke you were to be placed in a large, luxurious office originally intended for a person in a much higher position. It would suggest absurdity through its inappropriateness.

Planning to Improve Your Office

The planning process involves two interacting steps:

1. Develop a specific plan for projecting your personality and style.
2. Review the ways in which various aspects of an office can project character. Then plan physical changes that express the qualities you wish.

Pencil and paper are likely to be helpful in both steps. Actually writing down a list of the qualities you want to express will tend to sharpen your thinking about these matters. Keep your list around for a while, cross items out and add others. Talk it over with one or two friendly advisers who may offer suggestions or additions. Also, make a list of specific office furnishings you think might fit the purposes you have in mind. Above all, do not make hasty decisions about choosing a particular desk or color scheme before a logical, general plan has been drawn up.

Step I: Characterization

Compile a list of words that describe the character that you want your office to project. Take into consideration (1) your actual personal character; (2) the nature of your work; (3) the context in which your office will exist; (4) the flow of visitors; (5) the nature of the organization in which you work; and (6) your future plans. To start you off on this process, a list of words is provided here, arranged in alphabetical order. They may help you be more specific in describing your intentions.

Try to avoid thinking about terms as having "good" or "bad" implications. "Businesslike" or "efficient" tend to be thought of as good qualities for an office and "warm" is usually seen as more attractive than "cold," but these are generalizations. They are not necessarily applicable to any one particular situation. A marriage counselor may find it far more important to have an office that is welcoming, calm and reassuring than one that is "businesslike." Having a "warm" office may be quite inappropriate for the director of physical education at a military academy. Any quality may be right or wrong, depending on context. Also, do not worry about listing qualities that may seem contradictory. Most complex roles in modern life involve some paradoxes, and the multitude of design possibilities makes it possible to express contradictions effectively. An office can be both warm and businesslike, both calm and stimulating, through the right balance of elements that expresses both qualities. Give your list a little time to "season." Think about it off and on for a few days; add a term or cross one off as your thinking develops. Ask people whose opinions you respect for comments. When you feel content that the general program of intentions is right for you, you are ready for the next step.

This checklist of descriptive terms omits those that are so negative that they have no application—such as boring, depressing, dull, disorganized, and stupid. But it does include some ambiguous terms, like institutional and secretive, that can have either positive or negative connotations, depending on the context. Check the relevance of each term to your situation on the 0 to 5 scale. It may be interesting to ask other people, such as clients and colleagues, to try this on your behalf.

A careful reading of the charts and the check marks will provide you with a clear understanding of how your office appears and functions now. It can point up trouble spots that you might be able to alleviate. The goal is to determine how well your office does what you want it to do.

Office Evaluation Checklist

	Very Important	Important	Indifferent	Slightly Significant	Unimportant	Irrelevant
	5	4	3	2	1	0
Academic	___	___	___	___	___	___
Active	___	___	___	___	___	___
Adventurous	___	___	___	___	___	___
Aesthetic	___	___	___	___	___	___
Affluent	___	___	___	___	___	___
Artistic	___	___	___	___	___	___
Attractive	___	___	___	___	___	___
Austere	___	___	___	___	___	___
Avant-Garde	___	___	___	___	___	___
Bold	___	___	___	___	___	___
Bright	___	___	___	___	___	___
Businesslike	___	___	___	___	___	___
Calm	___	___	___	___	___	___
Caring	___	___	___	___	___	___
Cautious	___	___	___	___	___	___
Charming	___	___	___	___	___	___
Cheerful	___	___	___	___	___	___
Classical	___	___	___	___	___	___
Colorful	___	___	___	___	___	___
Comfortable	___	___	___	___	___	___
Conforming	___	___	___	___	___	___
Confidential	___	___	___	___	___	___
Contemplative	___	___	___	___	___	___
Cozy	___	___	___	___	___	___
Creative	___	___	___	___	___	___
Cute	___	___	___	___	___	___
Deep	___	___	___	___	___	___
Dignified	___	___	___	___	___	___
Dramatic	___	___	___	___	___	___
Eccentric	___	___	___	___	___	___
Economical	___	___	___	___	___	___
Efficient	___	___	___	___	___	___
Energetic	___	___	___	___	___	___
Exciting	___	___	___	___	___	___
Exclusive	___	___	___	___	___	___

Office Evaluation Checklist

	Very Important 5	Important 4	Indifferent 3	Slightly Significant 2	Unimportant 1	Irrelevant 0
Experimental	——	——	——	——	——	——
Fashionable	——	——	——	——	——	——
Feminine	——	——	——	——	——	——
Flexible	——	——	——	——	——	——
Formal	——	——	——	——	——	——
Futuristic	——	——	——	——	——	——
Generous	——	——	——	——	——	——
Guarded	——	——	——	——	——	——
Harmonious	——	——	——	——	——	——
Homelike	——	——	——	——	——	——
Imaginative	——	——	——	——	——	——
Impressive	——	——	——	——	——	——
Independent	——	——	——	——	——	——
Inspired	——	——	——	——	——	——
Institutional	——	——	——	——	——	——
Intellectual	——	——	——	——	——	——
Isolated	——	——	——	——	——	——
Learned	——	——	——	——	——	——
Light	——	——	——	——	——	——
Lighthearted	——	——	——	——	——	——
Lively	——	——	——	——	——	——
Luxurious	——	——	——	——	——	——
Masculine	——	——	——	——	——	——
Mechanical	——	——	——	——	——	——
Meditative	——	——	——	——	——	——
Musical	——	——	——	——	——	——
Natural	——	——	——	——	——	——
Old-Fashioned	——	——	——	——	——	——
Open	——	——	——	——	——	——
Orderly	——	——	——	——	——	——
Ordinary	——	——	——	——	——	——
Organized	——	——	——	——	——	——
Original	——	——	——	——	——	——
Peaceful	——	——	——	——	——	——

Office Evaluation Checklist

	Very Important 5	Important 4	Indifferent 3	Slightly Significant 2	Unimportant 1	Irrelevant 0
Playful	___	___	___	___	___	___
Posh	___	___	___	___	___	___
Powerful	___	___	___	___	___	___
Professional	___	___	___	___	___	___
Reasonable	___	___	___	___	___	___
Responsible	___	___	___	___	___	___
Relaxing	___	___	___	___	___	___
Restful	___	___	___	___	___	___
Routine	___	___	___	___	___	___
Rural	___	___	___	___	___	___
Safe	___	___	___	___	___	___
Scientific	___	___	___	___	___	___
Secretive	___	___	___	___	___	___
Sincere	___	___	___	___	___	___
Social	___	___	___	___	___	___
Sophisticated	___	___	___	___	___	___
Spacious	___	___	___	___	___	___
Startling	___	___	___	___	___	___
Stimulating	___	___	___	___	___	___
Straightforward	___	___	___	___	___	___
Strong	___	___	___	___	___	___
Studious	___	___	___	___	___	___
Stylish	___	___	___	___	___	___
Surprising	___	___	___	___	___	___
Systematic	___	___	___	___	___	___
Technical	___	___	___	___	___	___
Theatrical	___	___	___	___	___	___
Thoughtful	___	___	___	___	___	___
Traditional	___	___	___	___	___	___
Unique	___	___	___	___	___	___
Unusual	___	___	___	___	___	___
Urban	___	___	___	___	___	___
Youthful	___	___	___	___	___	___
Welcoming	___	___	___	___	___	___

Step II: From Intentions to Realities

Even in this step, do not rush to concepts that are *too* specific. Keep your selections of furnishings in words, not pictures or samples. Do not begin to select actual pieces of furniture or color swatches until you have gone through this step and have listed all the possibilities you can think of under each item heading. If the final project is to be put in professional hands, your designer should take over at that point. If you plan to follow through alone, gathering a large list of possibilities will help you avoid making piecemeal decisions. Be sure to put off specific and detailed planning until you have written down every idea you can come up with.

The following chapters describe the main elements of office design in terms of the character they project. Some of these elements you may not be able to change, even though they would project the qualities you desire, because you are limited by the realities of your situation. Do not be discouraged. When this happens, you must simply put more emphasis on using other elements that you *can* control to emphasize the right qualities.

The Individual Office

The person who is planning an individual office for his own business has a key decision to make—whether the office should be in his home or in a separate location. Each has advantages and disadvantages. At home you avoid the time and expense of commuting. You have the freedom to work at odd times (evenings, weekends) and can take advantage of conveniences your home offers, like storage facilities and a kitchen for making coffee. Providing your present home has extra space, you avoid paying office rent and can even take a tax deduction for that portion of your home used as an office, plus other business-related expenses. In this case, however, you should be sure that your office use meets IRS requirements. The disadvantages are that your work and home life may become tangled in ways that are not so desirable. You may feel that you never really leave the office, and its accessibility may draw you back to work in the evenings and on weekends when you would rather have free time. And you may find that home life introduces distractions that make you less efficient at your job.

A separate office in an office building, perhaps "downtown," can seem more businesslike and may make it easier to separate your private life from your work life. Against this you must balance the cost and time involved in commuting, the additional rent, phone bill, furniture, etc.

Ultimately, your decision will probably be based on the nature of your business and your own personality traits. If you have to work odd hours to meet deadlines, a home office might be best. But if you receive frequent vistors who react best to a business location, a business district office may be in order. You should evaluate your personality during this decision process, too. Are you systematic and orderly enough to work at home without distraction? Will you be lonely in an office without even a cat or dog for company? Also, think about your future plans. If they include expansion and the hiring of employees, a business location will serve you best. If you already have an office, you have probably answered these questions. But it may still be worth reviewing your situation to make sure that you have settled on the right decision.

There are also compromises possible, such as the "professional apartment," which is popular with some professional people, mainly doctors and dentists. It is laid out to combine office and living spaces with separate entrances and good internal isolation. Houses can be altered to provide a similar compromise. In any case, you should take the location of your residence into consideration. If you need to be in the financial district, a home office may be out of the question. But, if being in a residential area will help bring you work, a home office may be ideal.

One of the most important factors affecting the success of a home office is its location within the residence. The office should be sufficiently isolated from the rest of the dwelling so that family events do not interfere with your work. Business visitors should not bother your family and should not be too aware that they are, in fact, in your home. The location of entrances, hallways and doors, and sound barriers can deal with these issues if they are thought of in advance. It is also important not to slip into the frequent mistake of making the home office an afterthought in terms of location, layout and equipment. An office in the back of a garage with a worn-out desk and chair under a bare bulb hanging from a wire is not going to help you succeed. Many home offices reflect laziness or the desire to skimp, and neither one is a characteristic that suggests success orientation. On the other hand, if your home is attractive and interesting, and your office is too, the location may communicate your positive qualities in both office and private life. Most of us find it stimulating to visit an interesting person in their home office. The experience is positive if the home and office live up to our expectations. But if our expectations are not met, it can be depressing.

Think for a moment about what visitors are likely to come to your office. Perhaps only an occasional messenger will visit you, in which case visitors' reactions are not important. However, this is a very rare situation. Almost every office receives visitors, at least once in awhile. Frequency of visits is no indication of their importance. One visit a month or year by an important contact, such as a prospective client, may determine your level of success for a long time to come. One visit to "see the office" is a favorite preliminary check in the course of many business relationships. And what your office communicates during that visit can be vital in determining the turn of events for you.

If you have frequent visitors—clients, customers, patients or other people important to your career—the impression your office gives is even more significant. It also becomes a big factor in your decision to have an office at home or in a separate location. Your visitors' convenience may be as important as your own, and an office that is well planned and strategically located may be a definite requirement. The very idea that you are in complete control of the appearance of your office makes your visitors identify you with it all the more strongly. There is no boss or distant manager to blame for insufficiencies. This is not to say that there is any one "ideal" office situation. You must decide what will express your intentions strongly and honestly. This may be luxury and elaborateness in one kind of work, dignity in another, or simplicity and economy in a third. Your aim must be for an ideal match between your aims and intentions and the qualities that come across to a vistor. Remember that visitors recognize nuances in office design and transfer these slight variations into strong impressions. Almost everyone would be repelled by a dingy "hole-in-the-wall" office of a real estate salesman, because it shows that he does not deal in dependable buildings. A real estate office with paneled walls and thick carpeting would appeal to a person looking for first class property. But the same office might scare off more modest buyers.

Whether you have visitors often, seldom or never, you must remember that you, yourself, are an important visitor in the office. It is your own place, and you have made it what it is. It acts as a mirror of your personality, so the way you feel about your office is very likely to affect the way you feel about yourself. You can easily become used to any office situation, to the point that you hardly ever notice what it is like. Yet it influences you subtly each time you enter and all the time you spend in it. Even when you are away, the memory of it is sure to influence you in some way. If the office is dreary, messy, badly lit and cluttered with worn-out furniture, you can hardly fail to experience some sort of depression whenever you enter. You may not be conscious of it, but it says to you, "This is the sort of place that only a hopeless incompetent would tolerate." And that is hardly a success-oriented message. Such a message is bad enough when the office is provided by a firm, but when you know it is your own doing, it can weigh down your work life like a wet blanket.

The suitability of your office for you does not depend upon it being neat, modern, elegant or stylish. It depends upon how it supports your morale and self-determination. "Creative clutter" in an office can suggest interesting work and on-going projects, and can be stimulating. Odd or unusual furniture or equipment, like an old roll-top desk, or a piano in a corner of the room, may remind you of your unique character, independence and sense of self-direction. An unusual office, even worn and messy, may offer the comforts and satisfactions of an old shoe. In any case, your office should elevate your spirits whenever you enter, support you in your work, and stick in your memory as a place you want to go back to.

Practical matters are of importance, too, of course. Everything should be well-placed and convenient, work surfaces should be adequate and storage sufficient. You should not be bothered by interruptions or distracting noise. The goal is to combine these basic factors of efficiency with a setting that radiates your positive qualities and imprints them on the minds of your visitors.

The remaining issues pertaining to the individual office involve cost and how to think about paying for what you need. In an individual office there are no controls on expenditures, except those you set yourself. It is interesting that the same person who would complain about a firm's pinch-penny attitude toward office improvement, takes an even stingier point of view when it comes to setting up his own office for his own business. Often, the first office is a makeshift affair—usually because the enterprise is new and operating on a shoestring. This is a mistake, because it leads to negative thinking habits. While a corporation or large organization takes it for granted that the costs of adequate offices are part of the proper expenses of doing business, the solitary user usually views office expenses as a reduction in his earnings. This is a dangerous line of thinking because it tends to discourage investment in the very things that might support success. You must remember that investing in your office is, in fact, investing in yourself. If you do not have enough confidence in your abilities to invest in yourself, you will not succeed.

A large firm will supply even a junior typist with a modern electric typewriter of the best quality. But the solitary worker often tries to get by with a dilapidated machine that produces blurred bills and letters that take extra time and effort to type. In the same way, needed file cabinets are avoided while papers get hopelessly lost in untidy heaps. A broken floor lamp provides the only lighting, and the user wonders why he gets headaches.

Spending a lot is not always a route to better results, but spending too little almost guarantees poor results. The ideas of "return on investment" and "cost-benefit ratio" apply just as much to the individual office as to any in a larger organization. Rent, improvements, cost of furniture and equipment, and operating expenses such as phone, lighting, and air conditioning—all have an optimum expenditure level that delivers the highest benefit obtainable without waste. Probably the worst mistake of the individual office proprietor is to spend the least possible, which results in the least success. In the end, one can always remember that tax laws are set up to encourage expenditures that will aid your success.

The Office in an Organization

Planning office complexes for large corporations and governmental agencies has become a specialized profession outside the scope of this book. (However, we will review some typical approaches later on.) If your office is a part of a gigantic complex, you are hardly likely to undertake reworking the entire facility. You may feel, somewhat despairingly, that there is nothing you can do to improve the space assigned to you.

It is certainly true that your options and opportunities are more limited than those of the person who rents his own space. Still, the very limitations that organizations impose mean that small issues become relatively more important. Where everyone wears a gray flannel suit and white shirt, the color of a necktie becomes very important. Likewise, if office sizes and furnishings are rigidly standardized, choice of ashtray or picture frame can be highly meaningful.

Actually, few modern organizations impose restrictions that totally limit the development of office character. Rather, some standardization is chosen as a matter of organizational convenience. It is easier to order 100 identical desks than 100 different ones. The office user accepts what is provided without much thought as to how appropriate it might be for him.

In your own situation, you need to analyze what is possible now, and in the near and distant future. Then make plans to make your situation better than it is now, and a level above the norm for the offices of your peers. As a member of a large organization, it is particularly important for you to use your office as a lever for your own success. You cannot let it fall to the level of a mere practical necessity, because your indifference will create a drag on your advancement in the company.

First of all, consider where your organization stands within the "life cycle" of its office facilities. New offices tend to remain more or less as originally planned for a time. Later, however, changes and modifications creep in, layout and equipment become outmoded and the space becomes overcrowded. Finally, a new facility must be considered, planned and constructed. You can probably place your own office fairly accurately at a particular point in this cycle, which tends to run somewhere between 10 and 20 years. Of course, many offices are older, but these usually show signs of breakdown that is seriously damaging to the organization. The kind of possibilities that you can explore vary with the point in the office life cycle, and your planning should move with time to exploit possibilities as they open up. Let us take a look at the possibilities open to you in new, middle-aged and outmoded facilities.

New facility. You first need to assert your distinctive requirements and qualities in ways that are fully appropriate within the limits imposed by the organization. Very small things will tend to be significant, and will take special thought and care. A similar situation arises when you join an organization and move into an existing office. Make it yours in a positive way that will blot out the ghost of whoever occupied it previously, and make it clear that you are a strong and individualistic person.

Consider changing the furniture arrangement—even getting rid of a desk, and replacing it with a table, for example, if most offices in the group have desks. Introduce art works or appropriate objects of high quality that are attractive and easy to associate with your personality. Discard any routine or shoddy trivia—cheap, decorative wastebaskets and disposable ashtrays. At the same time, do not do anything outrageous. You may be very fond of your eight-foot-long mounted swordfish, but it has no relationship to your role in the organization and it will make you an office joke. The line between self-assertion of a favorable sort and behavior that will make you seem an eccentric is a fine one, and it is important to stay on the right side of that line.

Middle-aged facility. This office is settled, but still not outgrown. In this phase of the office life cycle, you need to watch out for two dangers. One is the risk that habit and adaptation will make you unaware that your office is becoming seedy. This is the time when upholstery gets shabby, walls become scuffed and fingerprinted, files fill up and cardboard boxes of folders stack up. This might be called the danger of creeping chaos, because it develops so naturally you do not notice it. But visitors see your office as a scene of incompetence and disarray. The second danger is that you can become the victim of skillful office territorial power maneuvers. As time goes by, changes take place. People leave and new people come in; people are asked to move to a "more convenient location." Crowding leads to people being doubled up in a single office.

When these changes take place, it is a perfect opportunity for playing territorial politics. Some people have an instinct for always needing to move to a more favorable location. They always find logical reasons to need more and better facilities. This classic office power game is won by those who are aggressive and aware. In this phase of the office life cycle, you need to fight creeping decline and chaos, but resist planned assault on the "office grabbers."

With controls and planning more relaxed in organizations, people are constantly striving for more prestigious offices. Your problem is to keep abreast of these tendencies without becoming an example of a power aggressor yourself, and leaving yourself open to criticism.

It is said that corner spaces are "powerful," in that they symbolize the ideas of protection from the rear, along with prestige of "visible amenity" (windows on two sides). And it is true that locations close to corner locations are likely to be closer to power, both literally and symbolically, than locations in the center of a row of spaces. Locations in the center of a sea of cubicles are obviously undesirable on any basis. You must be alert to the random moves that are occurring that affect you, and assert your requirements for beneficial change. At the same time, review your present situation with an eye to resisting the random decay that can reduce what was once a reasonable office situation to a laughable scene of confusion.

You will probably find that you have, in this phase of the office's life cycle, considerable freedom to make small changes in your work area. You may also be able to make changes within the realm of your authority, possibly extending to an entire department. Changes in desk or space assignments, rearrangement of furniture and equipment, and a new paint job may be helpful. Even careful management of minor items like bulletin boards, wall decorations and other accessories can maintain or better your office situation. Be alert to these possibilities, because being unaware of them will permit erosion of your position.

Outmoded facility. This is the last stage of the life cycle. The office has become overcrowded or its use has changed so drastically that it is obviously inappropriate and inefficient. People are sharing former private offices, big offices are used for minor functions, and some people are in remote "temporary" offices. The space—perhaps the whole building—looks old-fashioned and shabby. This is the scene in which the discussion of a new office begins. And this discussion is a signal to make moves that will help to assure that your spot in the new office will be right for you.

Express interest in participating in the planning of the new office. Don't appear interfering or agitate for your own self-interest alone. Express an honest interest in helping to make the new office right for all its functions. This will often lead to involvement at some level in a planning committee, or make you a spokesman for your department. It is not always the "boss" who is the most influential in planning the new office. Many decisions about when and how to move and how to plan the new office are made by groups and committees. So it is possible for you to offer input or actively participate in the planning process. Most office occupants are content to leave the planning to "them" and then grumble about the results. Expression of constructive interest is both unusual, and most often quite welcome.

From one to two years may elapse between the time when it becomes clear that a new office is required and the actual move. During this time, your role will depend upon your position in the company. If you are a key decision maker or a member of an official planning committee, you can make certain that the new office will be right for the company and yourself. The same applies if you are a spokesman for your department. Even if your role is less central, try to exert your influence in a positive way.

Large projects almost always require the services of professional planners and designers. Most often, an independent design firm is acquired, but sometimes the job goes to an in-house facilities planning department. The selection of the planning group is the key to the success of the whole project. Try to become familiar with the work of the planners being considered, and use your influence to steer the project to the best of them. A later chapter offers a briefing on the kinds of professionals that do office design and suggests how to deal with them. The more you know about this field, the more effective you will be in influencing the project in a constructive way. Professional office designers are usually quite aware of the efforts of various individuals and groups to maneuver for favorable situations, and discount their politicking. But the planners do need complete and accurate information, and often find it surprisingly hard to find in large complex organizations. Offer your help in every possible way that is appropriate. You might be able to do more than you think to have the project turn out well for you and the organization.

If you have a key role in the planning, you should make an effort to become something of an expert in office design. Reading this book is a good beginning, but read some or all of the professional design books listed in the bibliography at the back of this book. Also, read some of the magazines that deal with office planning and design. Professional office designers always find it a problem to communicate with executives who are involved in an office project for the first time. The more you know about the field, the better you can communicate, and the greater your influence will be.

In this phase, it is best to focus on the *whole* office and to avoid too much attention on your particular space. Office planners are used to people who profess general interest, but who really have their own self-interest in mind. And they find this type of scheming self-defeating. Concern with your own space is appropriate, of course, but only in proportion to its significance in the total project. If you are anxious to make sure you have some control over your own resulting space, press for this option for everyone. Sometimes management will allow everyone above a certain rank to ask for anything they want in their office space. One giant corporation allowed 40 vice presidents to specify any "style" office they might desire. The resulting chaos of such a situation is not helpful to either the individual or the organization. Urge top quality for every part of the organization, appropriate space for you and your work group, and seek personal expression through the means discussed in the following chapters.

When the new office is built, the life cycle begins again. If you have had a role in its development, you will identify with it—it will be yours totally, not just in terms of the space you occupy. Try to use this feeling as a basis to help whoever you can to adjust to its newness and make best use of the space. You may also choose to make an effort to slow the process of decline that gradually makes an office less attractive and efficient. There are offices that do not deteriorate over the years. One example is the corporate headquarters that Frank Lloyd Wright designed for the Johnson Wax Company in 1936. It is still a showplace more than 40 years later. For this kind of lasting quality, the project must have excellence to begin with, but management must also *insist* that the excellence of the office be maintained against the inroads of makeshift, clutter and decay.

Color and Texture

Color and texture are powerful tools for establishing character and atmosphere. Whole books are devoted to the meanings and uses of color, yet it remains difficult to pin down exact rules for color use in the complex situations with which design deals. One cannot, however, dismiss color as "all a matter of taste." Part of the impact colors have on people comes from deep physiological and psychological reactions that are inborn and unchanging. And part can be attributed to habits and customs that we all learn in a particular culture. Universally, it seems that red is exciting and black is depressing. But the association of black with death and mourning is cultural, because in China white is the color of death. Not only do individual colors project moods and meanings, but families of colors (warm or cool) and relationships of colors (contrasting, harmonious) have implications as well.

Textures are somewhat simpler to characterize as falling in a sequence from smooth to rough. Smooth textures suggest sophistication, elegance, style, and finish. Such words as "slick" or "polished" have both a literal and symbolic meaning that suggest this association. In general, smoothness is also regarded as "cold." In contrast, rough textures seem hearty, natural, homey and simple, and are associated with warmth. At an extreme, rough textures are seen as crude and uncouth. Each texture family is intensified when associated with related colors. For example, a shiny blue cabinet with chrome trim at one extreme, a shaggy brown rug on a natural plank floor at the other. Mixing opposite textures intensifies the effect of each, but leads to a total effect combining both sets of qualities.

The following lists colors by type, family, and specific name. It also gives some basic qualities that such colors tend to project. Although it is impossible to provide hard and fast rules that you can use to create a color scheme, the information should give you an idea of what to select and what to avoid in color when planning your office.

WARM COLORS, such as reds, oranges, yellows, and related browns and tans are associated with warmth, cordiality, cheer and generally favorable human qualities. They tend to seem "natural," although they are not the only colors of nature. Most natural materials used in building tend to have warm color tonalities.

REDS range from warm to hot, and are exciting and stimulating. They are also associated with tension and danger (heat and fire). Limited amounts of intense red can balance and augment blues and greens in a color scheme in a favorable way. If too much red and green are present in intense forms, however, painful tension can result.

ORANGES share the qualities of reds, but to a lesser extent. A red-orange color in intense, small quantities is a useful stimulant and modifier of otherwise neutral or cool color schemes.

YELLOWS are milder warm colors that are usually associated with cheerfulness and even humor. The brightness effect is strong, but the tendency toward excitement and tension is less than with reds. Yellow tints (beiges and creams) are "safe" colors having little negative implications, but tend toward insipidness when they are too diluted or overused. Yellows are the warm colors closest to the cool colors and are the least aggressive of "hot" colors.

GREENS are cool colors that are closest to the warm colors. A yellow-green can seem warmer than a clear blue. Greens are regarded as calm, peaceful, and constructive. In excess or in too great an intensity, however, they may be depressing. The restful qualities of green made them favorite colors of color systems of the 1930's, with the result that the monotonous use of dull greens has become associated with "institutional" color at its worst. Greens can be held in balance by small areas of intense red or red-orange, or with larger areas of red-browns.

BLUES are the coolest of colors. They suggest rest and repose, calm, and dignity. Overused, they generate depression and gloom. Reddish-orange colors offset the qualities of blues and can hold them in balance. Intense blues in small areas can accent and balance warmer color schemes.

VIOLETS and their darker versions, purples, are enigmatic and problematic colors. They are also on the borderline between warm and cool, but where greens seem to draw strength and stability from both warm and cool, violets seem to develop tension and instability. Violets are, therefore, "artistic" colors of sensitivity and sublety, but also have associations with ambiguity. In the deeper forms, called purple, the associations with tension and depression become stronger. This is a highly expressive color family, but one to be used with caution. As an accent, violet can balance and offset yellows.

COOL COLORS, such as greens, blues, and violets are, as a group, calming, dignified, and remote. They tend to be relaxing rather than stimulating, and depressive rather than exciting.

NEUTRAL COLORS, having no strong hue, include grays (warm and cool) and browns (more or less warm), and more dilute forms of brown called beige or tan. Neutral colors share the qualities of their more intense forms, but with less impact. They are staple materials of mild and gentle schemes and are often easiest to experience on a day-to-day basis. Dullness and drabness are possible negative impressions of neutral colors that need to be offset with small areas of intense, chromatic color. Browns and tans have a traditional association with masculinity and a sense of "clubby" relaxation. Browns and tans used in excess in institutional circumstances are associated with the worst of institutional drabness.

WHITE and near-white, very pale grays, and creams are technically neutral "non-colors" that suggest clear, bright openness. All white or near-white schemes tend to seem forced and empty. White, however, is never a "wrong" color and can be used in large areas with highly satisfactory effect if offset by small areas of intense, chromatic color. Outstanding schemes can result from large areas of white, lesser area of neutrals, and a few small spots of brilliant, intense color. This is a classic "high-style" formula.

BLACK and near-black colors are powerful accents that are depressing if used to excess. They imply dignity, stability, and solemnity. Extensive use of blacks is best confined to special-purpose space that is not occupied for extended periods (elevator cabs, vestibules, bathrooms). Bright, chromatic colors show up with great liveliness within a largely black setting.

METALLIC colors can be cool or warm. Chromium and stainless steel are "cold" with their mirror-like gleam. Brass, however, is a warm metallic, suggesting gold, and easily tends to be garish or vulgar if overused. Metallics are usually confined to accents and, when overused become overbearing and theatrical. Mirrors are a special case, but suggest a cold and glassy brilliance as they reflect whatever colors are present. Mirrors have an implication of fashionable but artificial pretension.

MONOCHROMATIC color schemes use only one color in a range of lights and darks and intensities. Harmony is guaranteed, but monotony is a danger. Such schemes tend to be somewhat artificial; they often do not wear well in daily experience. They are at their best when modified by some intense, contrasting color in small areas.

ANALOGOUS color schemes use a group of colors that are close together in the spectrum. Reds with red-violet and red-oranges would be an example. The closeness of the colors tends to insure harmony, but monotony is less of a risk. An analogous scheme, in which a great range of light and dark and intensity is present, can seem excitingly colorful. Accents in small areas chosen from a complementary color family are often helpful.

COMPLEMENTARY colors are pairs of colors from opposite sides of the familiar rainbow color wheel. The usual pairs are: red and green, orange and blue, and yellow and violet. When large areas from one family are present, particularly in pale or diluted form, a small area of intense complementary color lends liveliness and balance. Large areas of complementaries in near-equal area and intensity will produce hyperactive schemes that tend to clash. Intense complementaries placed close together will "vibrate" in a way that can be exciting.

CONTRASTING color schemes use complementary colors across the color wheel, but balance small areas of intense color on one side with larger areas of less-intense color on the other. If the colors on one side are spread over a portion of the color wheel, the term "split-complementary" scheme applies. A small area of intense red-orange on the warm side might, for example, be held in balance by larger areas of bluish-green and greenish-blue of lesser intensity from the opposite side of the wheel.

TINTS or pale colors result from diluting strong colors with white. Tints are often called "pastels." Individual names are sometimes applied, as with pink, the tint or pastel of red. Pastels seem mild, delicate, feminine, and if over-used, weak or childish.

SHADES are colors that are diluted and darkened with black or a complementary color. Dark shades can seem strong and rich when well used, but depressing and murky when overused. Dark and heavy color becomes depressing when not balanced by clear and lighter color.

TRIAD color schemes use the primary colors — red, yellow, and blue — to produce a so-called major triad, or secondary colors — orange, green, and violet — to produce a "minor" triad harmony. Although these are potentially highly effective and exciting color relationships, and favor-ites of painters, they are difficult to use in interior design and can, if they are out of balance, turn out to be garish and disturbing.

NATURAL color is the color of all materials which are left unpainted. They are finished only with preservative coatings such as wax or oil. Natural color is often an easy route to a highly successful look that tends to be soft, warm, and neutral. Most interior materials have natural colors in a range of whites, beiges, tans, browns, and red-browns. Used together, they relate well. Accents of red-orange or blue-green can intensify such schemes. Green plants, the most natural of materials, always work well as accents in such schemes.

Furniture

Because the furniture in your office is large, obvious and dominating, it usually is the prime factor in communicating your personality and your working style. Oddly enough, however, office furniture most often tends to be standardized. A steel desk with chromed legs and a walnut-finished top, like a gray flannel suit, communicates only that the user conforms to certain widely accepted standards. Giant corporations and bureaucratic agencies often urge such standardization in an effort to limit the scope of individual self-expression. By doing so, however, they limit individual incentive and give an impression of boredom. If your office is now equipped with standard, ugly, and boring furniture, and you want to make some changes (or if you are starting fresh), you should think about some of the possibilities that can pull your office out of the "routine" category and help make it a more special place.

A standard desk with two drawer pedestals, a desk chair, possibly one or two side chairs, plus a credenza and bookcase have come to be a standard office furniture package that probably rarely suits anyone exactly. But, just because it is so standard, this arrangement has become a formula that most people accept without a question and adapt to. Are desk drawers really the right storage space for you? Do you need more space, less space or perhaps a different kind of space? Is a desk really a better working surface than a table or a counter? Do you need more visitors' chairs—none at all?

A reasonable first step is to think a bit, without reference to your present office and its furniture, about what you do during a typical day and what equipment will serve your needs best. The following list includes many of the things that people do in an office; try estimating what percentage of your time you spend in each function:

Talking to a visitor
Talking to several visitors
Participating in a meeting or conference
Talking on the telephone
Dictating to a stenographer
Dictating to a machine
Writing by hand
Using a typewriter
Reading letters or memos
Reading magazines or books
Studying reports or statements
Checking and signing letters or memos
Sorting papers or documents
Looking up references
Drawing or sketching
Drafting
Examining objects or samples
Eating and drinking
Resting or napping
Listening to radio or other sound
Watching television
Thinking or meditating
Other _____

Think also about the physical position that best suits you for the activities that are important for you; for example:

Sitting upright
Sitting reclining
Standing
Pacing about
Lying down
Other _____

After you have considered all of the above, make a rough inventory of the things—not furniture—that you need at hand. Try to eliminate items you now have that would be better placed elsewhere. Files dating back a number of years, notebooks full of rarely consulted data, musty business books never read, and accumulated "gifts" are all likely to demand unnecessary storage space and to hide important things amid the clutter. Don't hesitate to add odd or unusual things that you really need or could use. For example, a songwriter might really need a piano, a film producer an editing table, a researcher a particular kind of microscope. With your needs fairly well defined, you are in a better position to consider your real furniture needs rather than stereotypes.

Primary Work Surface

Your primary work surface can be a desk top, of course; but consider whether a work table, possibly higher or lower than normal, might be better. A counter for either seated or standing work suits many kinds of activities even better than a desk does. A work table on wheels often is a convenience

The primary work surface of an office can be a desk, a table, or a built-in counter--whichever best suits the desired look of the office and the work to be done.

as either a primary or auxiliary work surface. A primary work surface that places you facing a wall—with desk or counter surface and shelving organized to suit your work needs—can be a very efficient arrangement that leaves floor space open for other activities.

Secondary Work Surfaces

An extra work top at one side, often lower than the main work surface, is often very convenient. It makes a good location for telephones, typewriter, calculator, and reference

Here the primary work surface is the projecting desk. The counter, which forms an L-shape surface, makes a good location for telephones, typewriter, and accessories.

material; the familiar L-shape of secretarial desks is a very convenient arrangement. Consider making the secondary unit a desk so that the primary unit can be a table. A special-purpose function (drawing or drafting, a CRT computer terminal) often can best be handled as a secondary work unit.

Conference Surface

If you spend a considerable amount of time talking to visitors or conducting meetings, a suitable table probably

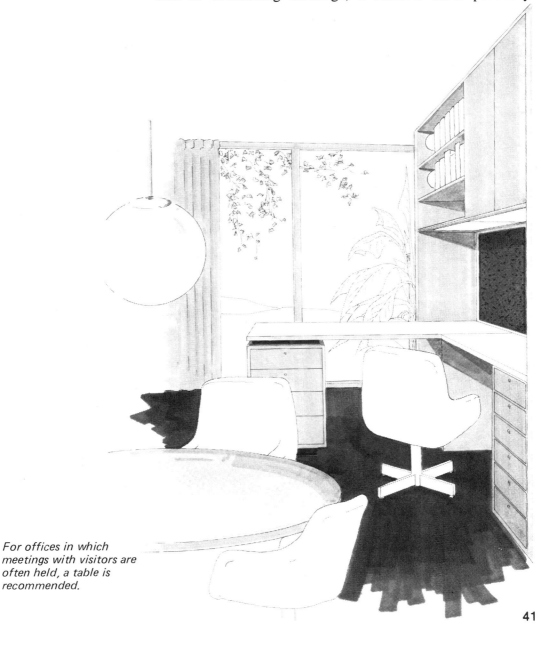

For offices in which meetings with visitors are often held, a table is recommended.

should take the place of a desk unit as the dominant furniture in your office. The standard desk is a compromise that leaves visitors talking across whatever material may be out in view or that forces you constantly to be putting away whatever you are dealing with at the moment in order to conduct an interview. Being the classic "clean desk man" requires constant effort or a staff or assistants always at hand.

Sitting upright across (or around) a table tends to establish a businesslike tone to conversation, neither unduly formal nor totally relaxed. Most desks with closed fronts establish a tone of distance and aloofness that makes meetings rather formal—possibly desirable if you want to establish your position of authority, but it often hinders easy communication. Round or oval tables further promote equality of communication because there is no "head of the table" to symbolize authority. In your own office (where you are "host"), you automatically have some degree of status, so you need not be afraid of making a table group *too* informal.

Primary Seating

Your chair obviously is an object of considerable importance to you; if you work seated much of the time, it is a major factor in your comfort and effectiveness. It is even an influence on physical health; poorly designed chairs are a significant factor in a whole range of ailments. Back disorders, varicose veins, and a variety of other circulatory and heart ailments can be caused or aggravated by the poor designs of many chairs. The large, thickly padded executive chair is likely to be a worse threat than the simple posture chair; even a hard stool is less likely to generate physical problems. Seek seating that offers some concern with the "human engineering" or "ergonomic" concerns of proper physiological support. Don't trust a quick estimate of comfort based on a minute or two of experimental sitting in a showroom. An illusion of instant comfort often goes with longer-term discomfort or with obscure problems of fatigue that may not be traced to a chair at all.

Many desk chairs offer adjustments for individual body size and shape and movements such as swiveling or tilting. Make sure that any adjustments are really set for your own needs. A poorly adjusted chair can be worse than a chair that is not adjustable. Many office chairs feature casters or rollers. Check how well the movement will work on the

Primarily, visitor's seating should be comfortable. Chairs that are light and small enough can be easily moved around the office. Also, visitor's chairs can be used as conference seating.

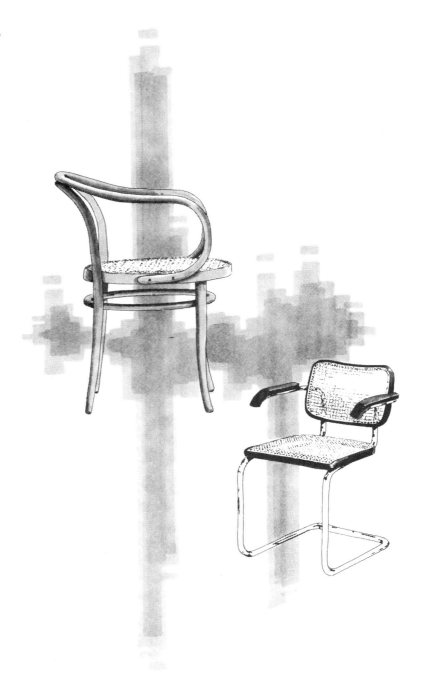

floor covering you plan to use. Wheels may bind on thick carpeting, making limited mobility and rapid carpet wear twin disadvantages.

The tradition of expressing status through chair size and luxury often works against good chair selection. Consider whether your own work patterns might not be best served by a simple and light chair that can be easily moved rather than the throne-like "judge's" chair so often selected for its appearance of grandeur.

Visitors' Seating

Seating for visitors is a less critical matter because visitors' chairs are only occupied for shorter periods and at intervals. You should attempt to make your visitors comfortable, but it is usually best to keep such chairs small and light so that easy movement is possible. Selection on the basis of appearance, provided that reasonable comfort is present, is logical. Visitors' chairs often will also serve as conference chairs.

Lounge Seating

If some or all of your meetings with visitors are informal, or if you want to make meetings less formal than they are now, a lounge seating group can be very helpful. But, remember that a lounge seating arrangement takes up considerable area. Cramming a minimal lounge group into a small office works against the sense of relaxation that is its purpose.

Lounge furniture usually is somewhat residential in character; it might, in fact, be identical to components sold for home use. Avoid seating that is so low that sitting down and standing up are awkard, and seating that forces visitors to assume awkard positions. Consider whether corner arrangements will generate inconvenient knee-bumping relationships at the corner. This is not a problem if ample lengths of sofa are provided, but it can be troublesome in situations where seating area is minimal. Try to look at lounge seating and desk and chair seating together to avoid height or scale relationships that might be awkard. Coffee tables and end tables need to be of heights and sizes that will not present tripping or bumping hazards.

Storage

General storage often is provided by desk drawers and credenzas or other similar storage units. This kind of box storage can be inefficient and inconvenient. The typical credenza usually contains items of little use or is jammed with notebooks and papers that only can be found after a long search from a stooped position. Consider what you really need to store, and try to provide minimal but adequate space

Storage-wall units, often European imports, provide custom-arranged storage and, if used as partitions, also have value as sound insulation.

at convenient locations. Wall-hung units or the panel-hung components of office systems tend to place storage where it is most convenient to use. Open shelves make things easier to find and usually discourage accumulations of old junk; such shelves also are economical.

Complete storage walls made up of prefabricated components are popular in Europe, particularly in Germany, and are available as imports. Units of this kind also can serve as partitioning between private spaces; they have good sound-insulating qualities and make storage available on both sides. This kind of storage system, however, has never become popular in the United States and remains expensive here due to the costs of importing such bulky units.

File cabinets and drawers, long the most dreary of standardized products, have been modified and improved by the introduction of "lateral filing," in which the drawers are wide and shallow, and the files are banked from side to side instead of from back to front. Lateral files generally are easier to use and better looking than conventional files and can, under some circumstances, be more space-efficient than old-fashioned storage units. Many office systems can incorporate files in ways that are neat in appearance, reducing the file-room dreariness associated with banks of green-colored cabinets. Files can be ordered in a wide range of colors and wood finishes to further combat the tendency to look bulky and depressing.

Floor Planning

After making decisions about the basic items you want to include in your office, you are ready to make a plan layout. Floor planning sounds technical, but it is not really difficult. Draw a plan, or have someone draw a plan for you, to scale. This means measuring your office with a tape measure or obtaining a plan from your building management or real estate agent. If you do the measuring yourself, note the dimensions on a rough sketch as you measure the space. If a plan is available, it will save you this chore, but the ready-made plan will probably be too small in scale for use. This will make it necessary to redraw it a larger scale.

Drawing to scale is an architect's method of showing large things in a convenient size while keeping all relationships in order. Favorite scales are 1/8 or 1/4 inch (1/8 or 1/4 inch equals one foot). The average office turns out rather small at either of these scales. For one private space, 1/2-inch scale may be better. In any case, the idea is to draw the space so that every actual foot is represented by a fraction of an inch. You can buy an "architects scale" ruler for this purpose or use graph paper with 1/4-inch squares to save time. Doors, windows, and furniture are then drawn on the plan to the same scale so that you can see how everything will fit.

To make a floor plan layout, measure the office space, and then make a rough sketch, noting the measurements.

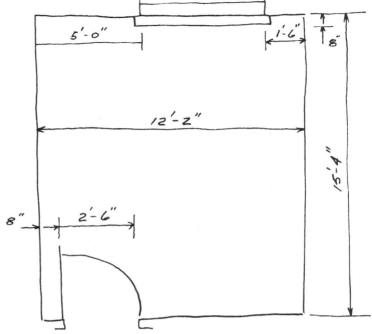

A scale drawing will prove very useful. Each foot of office space can be drawn as a 1/4-inch, for example, providing a realistic view of the area available. A convenient way to draw a layout to scale is to use graph paper marked off with 1/4-inch squares that can depict any measurement desired--for instance, one square per foot.

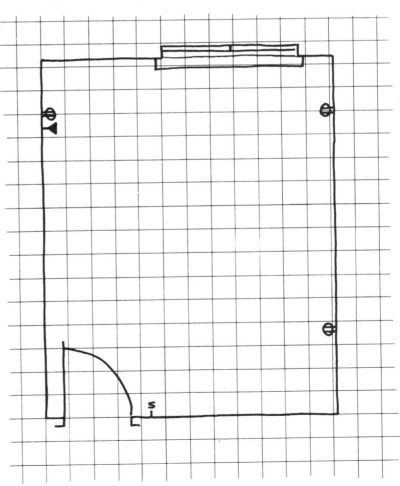

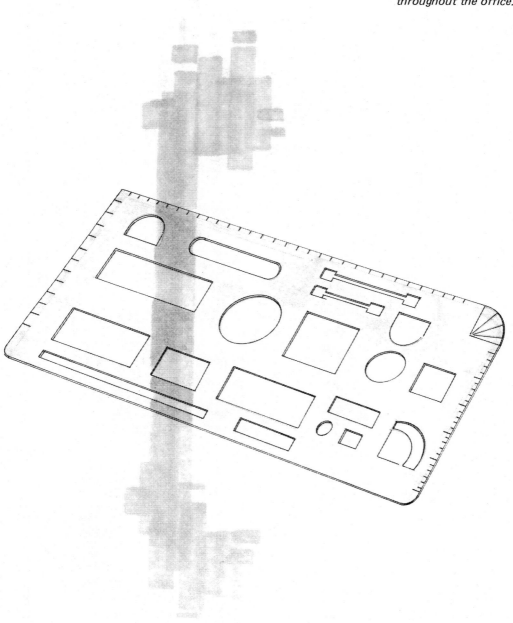

A furniture template, specially designed for making sketches of floor plans, is useful in planning the placement of furnishings throughout the office.

A straightedge will be useful in making scale drawings if you use a T-square and triangles. Put a piece of tracing paper over your basic plan (walls, doors, and windows only) and draw a furniture layout on the tracing paper. A template for drawing furniture can be found in a drafting supply store; such a template can be helpful, but it is not necessary if you measure in scale to get the sizes of things correct.

Do not expect your first rough plan on the tracing pad to work out—it is a first trial that you will want to revise again and again. It is often handy to cut out scale drawings of the furniture items you plan to include from cardboard or heavy paper so that they can be pushed around on your plan to try various arrangements quickly. You can use the furniture template to make the shapes for the cutouts.

Such a template has cut-out shapes representing chairs (the U shapes), and primary and secondary work surfaces (rectangles). Wavy lines can be drawn in by hand to represent drapery.

As you plan, try to think about how each arrangement will look and feel. Think about how you will feel and what you will see when you are seated in your office. What will visitors see as they enter and after they are seated? How will you and they move about, in and out, to seats, closets, etc., without awkward turns or bumping into furniture? Who will face the windows and how will it seem in the morning, at midday, and in the late afternoon? As you settle on a plan you think will work well, draw it out carefully and keep it around for a few days while you continue to think about it and imagine living in it. Show it to a few people whose opinions you value and listen to their comments without being too quick to accept their suggestions. As you develop your floor plan, keep the following suggestions in mind:

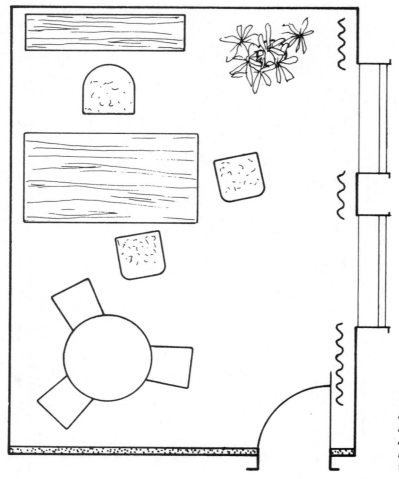

This office layout shows a conference table (circle) and the seating positions around it. Always indicate doors and windows in a plan.

An L-shaped desk and
seating for two visitors
can be designated on a
floorplan, as well as
large accessories such
as plants. In this way,
the traffic flow through
the office can be planned.

For a desk-less office, a
round table might be
chosen as the primary
work surface. Other
details of the office
design such as cork walls
(dotted border at left of
sketch) can also be included
in the drawing.

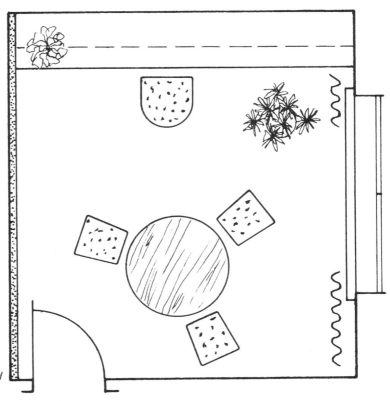

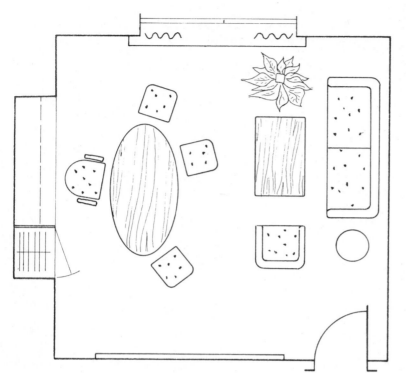

The plan might call for an elliptical primary work surface with a secondary surface behind it (rectangle with dotted line), and lounge seating which might include a couch.

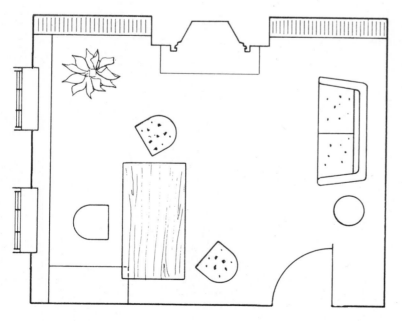

An office in a converted residential space might contain such things as a fireplace and mantel (top center), and surrounding bookshelves (long rectangles with vertical lines.

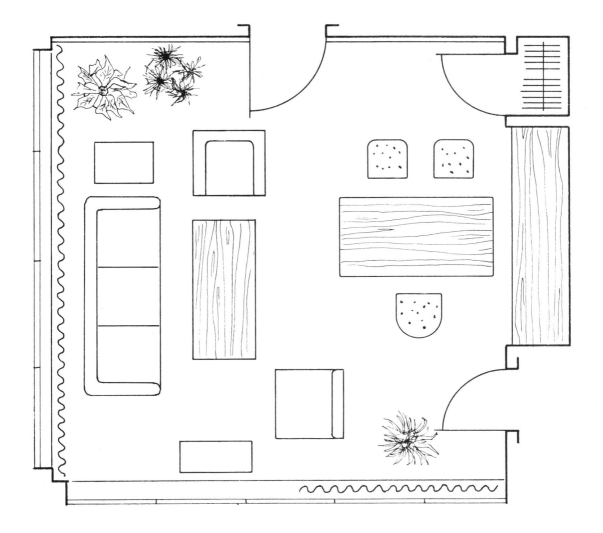

A spacious office might include lounge seating for five, several doors—perhaps to private washrooms and large closets—and a work counter as well as a large desk.

1. Do not feel that everything must be exactly balanced or on center unless you are trying for a *very* stiff and formal office.
2. Do not place seating for people who will talk together in such a way as to keep them too far apart or at uncomfortable angles to one another. Do not place anything important (desk or sofa) diagonally in or near a corner.
3. Do not leave vast empty spaces between items of furniture even if you have space to spare.
4. Sketch in lines to show the pathways that you and visitors will take when moving into and out of the office. If these traffic patterns seem complex and confused, try making some changes to make the patterns more simple and logical.
5. Try not to crowd the plan. If the items you are including

are hard to fit in, try to omit some items or to find smaller versions.

6. If one or more walls have a special treatment (paneling, tackboard, fabric covering), show it with a double line or a color. Show the general way windows or other glass area will be treated. Remember that drapery or blinds can extend beyond a window.

7. Consider whether any built-in units will be helpful, and show these on your plan. A radiator enclosure, a storage wall with shelves, and cabinets are typical examples.

Once you have a plan that satisfies you, draw it a bit more carefully on a fresh sheet of tracing paper and have a few copies made on a copy machine. This is now your basic document to guide the next steps. You can still revise it, of course, but keep it up to date to show any revisions that you may decide upon.

Furniture and Equipment Selection

The floor plan you have drawn probably shows only a desk, chairs, a sofa and other items in a general way. It is now time to move to specifics. Make a list of the furnishings included in the floor plan, perhaps giving each a letter or number. Anything that you already have and will be keeping should be noted and identified. Anything that must be purchased new should be selected, and listed by source, model number, etc., so that you can place orders in a methodical way. In some cases, you may have to go back and change your plan if the item you select is different in size and shape from what you drew—a larger or smaller or oval desk, for example. Beware of selecting larger items without changing the plan—it can lead to unpleasant surprises.

How to find the new items you may need is covered later, but notice here that it is wise to keep a catalog sheet or picture of each item all together in a folder. Write a memo for each piece of work to be done ("carpet floor," "make draperies," "build special cabinet," for examples) and keep it in the folder with notes on who will do each job, and when. Make a special memo for lighting and note how this will be dealt with. You may want to make an extra ceiling plan to show new or changed lights in the ceiling. List any electrical items (outlets, switches) in a memo and itemize the installations that must be made by an electrician. Also, include a memo for any telephone installation work needed. You may be surprised at how many items of detail pile up. It may be wise to pass this "work-folder" on to an assistant or secretary to follow up if you are likely to be too busy to deal with it all as time goes on.

Color, Material, and Finish Selection

At first glance, coordinating the surfaces of your office might seem easy and fun, but doing it methodically to get everything together in sample form at one place and time is the most vital of professional tricks. If you order a desk in "walnut" on the telephone, select a carpet in one showroom, choose upholstery fabrics in another, and give a painter a color sample at a different time, the chances are that some or all of these things will not seem right when the job is done. Human vision and memory are simply not sufficiently precise about such things to make it possible to coordinate a decorative scheme in this way.

For each item that you are considering, get a sample or some alternative samples and spread these all out on a desk or table, grouped together so that they touch. Start with the items where there is limited choice—wood finish and floor covering, for examples—and then add textiles and paint colors. Colored papers are handy for simulating paint colors. Look at the whole color scheme under the kind of light that you will be using—daylight, incandescent, fluorescent, or a mixture.

Add in bits of colored paper to suggest small colorful accessories if they will be significant. If this color scheme of small samples looks attractive and right to you, and if it has the character you are seeking, you will almost certainly be satisfied with the final result. Paste the samples of your final selections on a board and keep it as a record. Be certain, if any substitutions have to be made, that a sample of the item is checked against this board and glued down in its proper place.

When all the colors and finishes have been established on this coordinated chart, go back to your folder of furniture and other items. Add to each selection the data on color and finish. It is this methodical way of being sure that all colors and finishes interrelate that will protect you against the erratic and slap-dash kind of color that results from amateur decoration schemes.

If you are only making minor revisions in an existing office that is generally satisfactory, you can use the office itself, as it is now, as your color-coordination device. Remove or cover over any items that are unsatisfactory in color or finish, and study what remains visually. Hold up samples or squares of colored paper in the space to represent possible changes or additions. Perhaps you can get a larger sample to represent a new carpet or a reupholstered piece of furniture. The principle is still the same—try to have *every* item present at the same time and place while you study how the effect supports the aims that you have established in your program.

Once you have a color plan in this way, you can order needed items and professional work with some confidence that everything will work out well in the completed project. Stick to your plan as the new elements begin to arrive. If walls are painted first or new carpeting is laid before other changes come through, the isolated items may not look right. Don't lose your nerve and begin making spur-of-the-moment changes. Wait until everything is in place to evaluate the result. Colors influence one another, and a wall color that looks all wrong when it is the only new item might take its place perfectly when the other new items arrive that relate to it.

Locating Sources

In making your selection of furniture and the materials and colors related to furniture, you will have to confront the problems of discovering what is available and finding what you want. If you are to avoid the formula solutions of desk/chair/credenza in routine finishes, you will have to do some searching and exploring. There are a vast number of office furniture manufacturers in the United States and abroad, each with a varied and complex range of products, and many items not usually considered to be "office furniture" are perfectly suited for office use. Unfortunately, the typical office furniture store only has space for a handful of items in its showroom and naturally tends to display the routine products that are most in demand. To avoid drifting into dullness, try any or all of the following:

1. Write away for literature from manufacturers whose products interest you. Many are listed in this book; other names can be found in business and interior design magazines. Do not expect to receive complete catalogs, but the brochures available will give you an idea of what is available.

2. Most major manufacturers have showrooms in the larger cities. Although you cannot order there, you can study the actual furniture, obtain literature and make notes of the stock numbers of items that interest you. While at the

showroom, obtain the name of the dealer nearest you who distributes this manufacturer's products. Remember that it is easiest to order furniture in the materials, colors, and finishes that are "standard" in a given product line, so collect samples and swatches where there are choices.

3. Once you know what you want and have the name of the appropriate dealer, he will be happy to take your order and arrange for delivery, even if you are asking for an item that he does not ordinarily carry. Larger dealers usually have a good library of catalogs, as well as color and finish samples. The dealer can be quite helpful in this respect. Discourage his efforts to switch your interest to items in stock unless you really prefer them.

4. Explore non-office furniture. There is no reason why a desk chair must always be a massive swivel-tilt product on casters. A light caned, bentwood chair might suit you much better, will certainly cost less, and can be found in a department store, furniture store, or in one of the "good design" shops that cater to homemakers. A flush door from a lumber yard mounted on simple legs (available over the counter) makes an excellent table-desk and a small file unit or artist's taboret stand may be all the storage space needed.

5. Look for secondhand or antique office furniture if you find it interesting. Battered routine furniture of a few years back will not help, but a roll-top desk from the 1880s in "golden oak" can be beautifully refinished and provides marvelous work and storage space. Unfortunately, such items, worth almost nothing a few years ago, are being "discovered" as antiques with correspondingly escalating prices; but there are still bargains to be found. If you are interested in genuine antiques, you probably already know that prices can be staggering and that search, selection, and purchase can be a long and difficult process. But it is a process that many people seem to enjoy as a hobby, and you can always excuse the high prices by noting that an investment in antiques is almost sure to appreciate. Good-quality reproductions of antique designs are available from a few manufacturers (also at high prices), but beware of cheap and shoddy "period" furniture that is only a feeble imitation of the real thing.

Furniture Style

When considering antique or reproduction antique furniture, you will have to think a bit about furniture styles, how they can best be used and what they are likely to project about your personal style. Fine antiques almost always look attractive when placed in a simple modern room setting with ample space around them. Antique chairs can, for example, look very good around a modern table as long as size and height are appropriate. If your office has period character, you may want to choose related furniture; this is not essential, however, since good modern furniture can look very fine in a period setting. Trying to create a "period office" in a modern setting is more difficult. It is not always successful, is always expensive, and it sometimes leads to ludicrous results.

Mixing styles, which often is suggested by professional decorators, is also a precarious route to take. It takes a very special talent to put together objects from a wide range of times and places without awkward clashes resulting. Always remember that your aim is to say something about yourself through the design of your office. If you are considering exploring the possibilities of a particular style in furniture, the following list will give you some idea of what images the best known styles tend to project.

CLASSICAL (Roman and Greek) styles are associated with dignity, authority and tradition. They turn up as the styles of Federal and other older governmental buildings, bank buildings, and some older office buildings. "Landmark" status often goes with fine buildings of this sort. Interiors often include details that evoke the Georgian or Federal periods of American architecture. This is a monumental style and is at its best in support of dignity and power.

GOTHIC AND TUDOR styles are almost exclusively associated with academic and religious institutions. The atmosphere is likely to be "warmer" and closer to a residential feeling than in classical buildings. Power and authority are sensed as secondary to the dominant characteristics of tradition and conservatism.

GEORGIAN design is what most people identify with Colonial Williamsburg. This is a style that has a certain sense of residential warmth and comfort along with projections of tradition of the most conventional and conservative sort. It has been a favorite style for the offices of prestigious law firms, insurance companies, and firms of accountants. The tendency to suggest conservatism is now, as time moves along, becoming a leaning toward stodginess, which can be dangerous. Bad imitations of Georgian furniture and Georgian details (paneling, fireplaces, etc.) abound in second-rate restaurants and in offices that make half-hearted efforts at "class." The Georgian interior is only impressive at its very best (and therefore most expensive) and will still suggest an emphasis on the past, rather than the present or future.

COLONIAL design is an overworked term that has tended to become meaningless with overuse. It should refer to early American practice (pre-1776), having something in common with Georgian style but with a simplicity and modesty best related to residential use. Most often, the term is simply a vague designation for some version of Georgian design. A truly "colonial" office is hardly a realistic possibility unless it has a totally residential character. Simplicity and coziness are the usual associations.

VICTORIAN design, notable for excessive richness of ornament and for dark and often dismal spaces, has had a history of rejection during the first half of this century. However, it has found a new audience as historic preservation has come to attention. There are associations with the development of American industry in the nineteenth century and the development of the West that can make real Victorian spaces and objects charming and stimulating. The flavor tends to be personal, even eccentric. The roll-top desk is a key theme in the Victorian office. It is a style worthy of preservation, but almost certain to seem false and artificial in reproduction.

FRENCH design periods most often talked about are those of the kings Louis XIV, XV, and XVI. The themes of pretension, elaborateness, and "high style" are associated with this kind of design that is, by nature, not well-related to office use. There are implications of extreme luxury and expense and of an artificial and aristocratic orientation. Occasional use in office design usually is connected with style-oriented fields, such as fashion or cosmetics, with overtones of femininity and ostentatious lavishness. Formality is also a dominant theme, but it is the formality of the aristocratic dwelling.

"French Provincial" refers to the French styles that were modest adaptations of aristocratic French periods. These are residential styles with little applicability to office spaces. Most design bearing this label is so synthetic as not to justify any label at all except "fake."

SPANISH styles, based in Renaissance tradition, are associated with the American Southwest and with California and Florida locations. They were favorite styles of the 1920s, with implications of association with Hollywood and Florida millionaire life-styles. There can be a sense of asso-

ciated charm and history in genuine contexts, but taken out of appropriate location and genuine surroundings, these styles become painfully artificial.

MODERN design is most often thought of as non-stylistic—that is, simply contemporary and direct. Modernism has now been around long enough, however, to have developed subcategories of recognizable style differentiation. Some of those subcategories are Bauhaus, Art Deco, and High Tech.

Bauhaus style, emphasizing chrome tubing, white walls and primary colors, is usually felt to be cold and clinical, but highly aesthetic and a touch futuristic in spite of its 1920s origins. It is currently a "high style" with implications of elegance, culture, and artistic concern.

Art Deco is the current term for the style of the 1930s that emphasized rounded corners, zig-zag motifs, and the streamlining beloved by industrial designers. Dropped in the 1940s and 1950s as outmoded, it is now very popular. Associations are with style-oriented activities and pretensions.

High Tech is a new orientation in modern design concerned with elements borrowed from advanced technologies in industry, aviation, and space exploration. The character is cold but exciting, a bit artificial and style oriented, but futuristic and progressive in implication.

The risk in all uses of a "style" is that the dominant idea projected is likely to be one of artificiality, pretension, and ostentation. Qualities such as honesty, directness, simplicity, and sincerity are best conveyed where style for its own sake has been forgotten and truly personal style takes over in place of a pose generated out of rule books for decorators. Things that are real, like old buildings and interiors, antique furniture or new furniture, have the ability to generate the space that you want and need. Imitations, however carefully "styled," have a way of implying insincerity.

Fakery, in fact, is an element in so much design that it deserves a word of its own. There are endless catalogs filled with products that fake one or another supposedly desirable element of the office interior. One can buy new "Georgian" desks and "Chippendale" chairs, knotty pine "Colonial" file cabinets and telephone enclosures, electrified oil lamps and candelabra, pre-finished plastic walnut wall paneling, machine made oriental rugs, and similar items endlessly. No one has offered a knotty-pine typewriter, nor a Lear jet disguised as a couch-and-four, but that is probably only because the idea has not yet occurred to anyone. Even the

Desks of French Provincial design are better suited to residential application than to offices. Sometimes such furniture in an office context suggests fakery.

most convincing imitations project a sense of their falsity, even if only at a subliminal level. Avoid art reproductions, antique furniture reproductions, imitation wood-grain panels, imitation marble, and all such tastelessness. A simple and modest office with inexpensive but real contents can be convincing and impressive, while an elaborate stage-set of fakes always suggests that the occupant is synthetic as well.

Quality

Quality of office furniture varies over a wide range but is not hard to evaluate. This is a highly competitive field in which the various manufacturers try hard for competitive prices. As a result, price is a fairly good index to product quality. Salesmen and dealers will usually be glad to explain why one file cabinet or desk, outwardly similar to another, is more expensive, and the explanations will usually be quite realistic. Bottom price levels are achieved by leaving out features (ball-bearing drawer slides, height and tilt adjustments of chairs, for examples) and by using inexpensive materials and finishes. It is not hard to see the difference between a fine wood veneer and a cheap plastic imitation if they are placed side by side. Quality of paint finishes and plating on metal is harder to assess visually, but will follow comparable patterns. Open and close doors and drawers, look behind and underneath for construction details, shake and bounce parts, bounce in seating, roll around in chairs on casters. You will sense a level of quality that will probably be quite accurate. You will have to decide on the quality level that is right for your needs, but remember that first price is only one aspect of cost. A $45 chair that falls apart in a year is not, in the end, cheaper than a $300 chair that is still usable after ten years. And the higher-priced one may deliver more satisfaction during those longer years of its life.

The furniture business is always beset by the problem of "knock-offs," cheap imitations of well-known and popular products produced to cut into the sales of the originals that they imitate. The makers of these imitations often cut their costs by skimping on showroom space, advertising, and catalogs, and they may offer their dealers less advantageous terms than the suppliers of the original, more costly, products. If this makes it possible for you to find genuine bargains, there is no reason not to take advantage of it, but beware that look-alike products can be quite different in quality. The knock-off is often an import, manufactured where cheap labor and materials are available but where quality controls may be lacking. A certain well-designed steel tube and leather chair is available from a major manufacturer, for example, or from a knock-off source for about one-third the price. The cheap chair uses self-tapping screws with ugly heads in place of the neat machine screws that run into threaded holes in the original. The chrome plate on both chairs looks the same when new, but in a few years the finish on the knock-off may turn to rust. The quality of the leather, thread and stitching are obviously inferior when the two are placed side by side. When confronted by such comparisons, you have to decide whether the extra cost of the authentic version is worthwhile in your planned use.

Imported Furniture

Imported office furniture of interesting and unusual design is regularly available from certain showrooms and dealers. Quality is variable, but often very high, and adventurous designs that might not be offered by a manufacturer in the United States often turn up. For many years, imports were also generally good bargains, but changes in economic conditions have wiped out that advantage to a large extent and have even made imports from some countries excessively expensive. The areas of origin of most interest are Scandinavia, Germany, Switzerland, Italy, and Canada.

Among the Scandinavian countries, Denmark has a long tradition of furniture design and craftsmanship in the generally contemporary mode called "Danish modern." The low prices of a few years back have disappeared, but work of certain famous designers continues to be available. Hans Wegner, Fritz Hansen, and Arne Jacobsen are well-known Danish designers who have developed outstanding office furniture. Swedish and Finnish designs also are of interest in some cases. The molded plywood furniture of Alvar Aalto is particularly well-known, but because of its Finnish origin, has become relatively expensive.

German office furniture is usually of superb technical quality, but is seldom imported because of its high price and generally unexciting design. There are exceptions in well-engineered storage systems, such as the puristic and elegant designs of Dieter Rams.

Swiss products share the quality and high price of German imports and may seem rather cold and technological to many Americans. Fritz Haller, Robert Haussmann, and Hans Eichenberger are distinguished Swiss designers.

Italy remains a source for lively and economically priced furniture products, lamps, and accessories. Italian design tends to be adventurous, distinctive and avante-garde in tone. Mario Bellini is the designer of one widely recognized office system, Bob Noorda of another.

Canada is also a source of a number of office furniture product lines of good quality. Canadian products are very similar to those of the United States.

The problems that are always a source of some concern in considering imported furniture have to do with reliability of delivery, repairs and service, and continued availability of matching components over a period of years. As with foreign cars, some imports have been available briefly and then have disappeared. Problems of dock strikes, currency fluctuations, and similar vagaries all can be problems. In general, if you spot imported items that are available from an American importer having a good reputation for reliability, and if you expect your order to take care of your needs for years to come, there is no reason not to choose anything of this kind that suits you.

Office Systems

Open planning (or office landscape, as it is often called) presents some special furniture problems, since furniture must take over all of the privacy functions that walls and doors provide in conventional offices. In an effort to solve that problem, office furniture manufacturers have developed a number of "systems" in which panels of "work station" elements screen each office area from its neighbors. If your office is part of an open plan group, you will want to investigate the various systems available, or explore the possibilities of the present system used in your office. Generally speaking, great flexibility is possible with open office systems and you may find that it is easier to "personalize" your space with this kind of furniture than with more conventional types.

If your office is a conventional type (with walls and a door) do not dismiss the open plan systems as possible sources for individual elements that can work very well in regular offices. Work station groupings developed for open plan use can be used as alternatives to a conventional desk-credenza setup — possibly much better suited to your way of working.

In the award-winning office designed for an official of a self-improvement organization, an interior skylight is used. It makes the pitched-roof office compatible with the building's hung-ceiling general office area. Up-lights at the base of the skylight illuminate the ceiling, as do fluorescents on the top of the hollow beam, which contains track lighting.

Successful Offices –
A Color Portfolio

The sleek design and the durability of the materials used throughout this award-winning office (left and upper right) suggest success, stability, and competence. The space is divided through furniture arrangement into work, conference, and lounge areas. The desk (right) and conference table (left) were custom-made, as was the carpet.

With a primary work area to one side and a central conference table, the occupant of this office (right) can conduct brief meetings from his desk. Large, movable oak storage modules accommodate a great number of confidential files. The paneling and table top are also oak.

A corporate executive, working with his company's interior design department, planned wisely and incorporated a great deal of storage space into his 15x20-foot office. The cabinetry behind the desk was custom designed for display as well as storage, and to provide a suitable area for the photographic mural above it. Since the company's furniture is standardized, personalization comes from the use of art objects like the mural and wall hanging.

The large wall cabinet used in this attractive, well organized office, which measures only 15x15-feet, provides abundant storage space while maintaining an uncluttered look. The top of the cabinet is a perfect place for plants.

The work space of a
chairman of the board
pivots around a burl desk
and side credenza, which
contains roll-out dictation
equipment and intercom.
They form an L-shaped
work and formal
conference area. A
pedestal table
accommodates informal
conferences. An Eames
lounge chair provides
comfortable seating for
the reading of reports.
The office's wall paneling
is teak. Similar paneling
conceals a large storage
area (not shown).

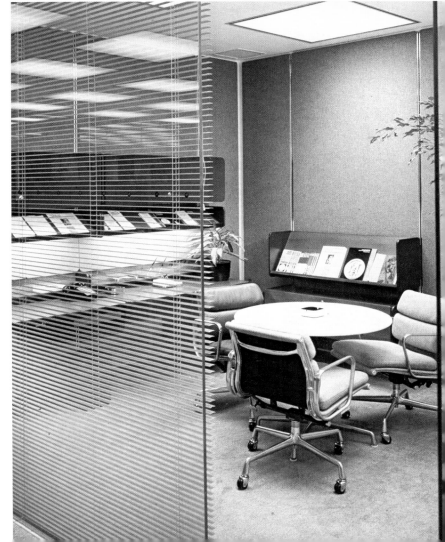

A bank manager's office,
though small, is used for
heavy client contact. So
the 12x12-foot space
incorporates a conference
area composed of a white
marble-top table and
comfortable chairs.
Blinds over the glass
partition maintain an open
look while providing
privacy when needed. The
floor covering is square
tile carpeting.

Low-key elegance is
created through the use
of rich woods and
textures (left and top
right). Shutters are
built of weathered barn
wood. Under the main
chair is brick paving tile.
The eclectic use of wall
art and accessories,
mostly personal items of
the executive, adds to the
overall elegant effect.

A jewelry company
president uses a
conventional desk plus
a credenza (right)
because he does a great
deal of paperwork in his
10x12-foot office. A
pedestal table is used for
meetings with clients.
The mirrored cabinet
holds large jewelry cases.
Because this jewelry is
examined regularly, both
fluorescent and
incandescent lighting
are provided.

In a 13x17-foot management office (left), a table centrally located in front of the task-lighted counter and a rolling file (under the table) are often used to create a large L-shaped work area. A space can be created by moving the table across the room. The plentiful tackboard areas are used for the display of work-related graphics.

A lawyer uses a marble desk top in his 15x18-foot office for discussions with clients. The inclusion of a credenza allows the conference area to remain uncluttered. Original, refinished wood flooring borders the oriental rug.

A bank president, due to high client contact, wanted two conference areas (right). The first surrounds a rosewood desk with mohair upholstered chairs. The second area, less formal, includes a textured wool carpet and armchairs. Drapes can be drawn over the tinted-glass partition for complete privacy. A sliding wood entry door next to the desk provides privacy.

An executive of a television station wanted his office style to reflect the station's efficiency. The pedestal table serves as the conference area; the work station is strategically located in the extreme corner of the trapezoidal space, which measures approximately 9x11-feet.

The arrangement of an attorney's office emphasizes client conferences in relaxed, dignified surroundings. The focal point of the 15x18-foot room is the table-desk, covered in leather. An Oriental rug is used to add color while allowing the attractive wood flooring to show.

Traditional is the look of this office, created for the president of a design firm. Wood is used for the cabinets and walls. The cabinetry behind the petite Granette-topped desk (custom designed) opens to reveal work surfaces, tackboard walls, and storage -- helping to maximize the versatility of the 11-1/2x14-foot office. The ceiling treatment is Belgian Linen velvet.

The office of a design firm executive eliminates clutter while providing ample work space in an area measuring only 11-1/2x14 feet. Solid teak shutters conceal the work area behind the marble-top desk. It contains files, a drawing board, a bookcase, and cork walls. Teak flooring material is used on the walls and ceiling. Built into the desk are intercom, phone, dictation equipment, and lighting and drapery controls.

A 13x16-foot office layout designed for meetings involving large-scale architectural plans is dominated by a large table (right). The table has a distinctive inset of virtually indestructable orange lacquer. The work station locks, but no hardware is visible.

A cultural center director's office (left) which measures 12x18-feet makes use of components that were selected so as not to compete with existing features such as the marble fireplace, wood paneling, and large window. Because of the southern exposure and the pleasant view, the windows are left bare. The lighting is indirect, from fixtures on the fireplace side of the room.

The 15x20-foot work area of an industry executive was planned for a high-quality look and to accommodate frequent inter-office conferences. Attractive accessories like the in-box and desk clock add to the well-tailored effect. The carpeting is wool.

The open floor area, covered by an antique Oriental rug, provides space in this 18x18-foot office for laying out large market chart books. The black cube to the left contains telephone; word processing terminal; electronic dictation machine; and controls for drapery, sliding entry door, and private elevator. The ceiling fixtures have fresnel lenses and are controlled by rheostat for diffused, variable lighting.

A study in contrasts is the best way to describe the 13x17-foot office of a Southwestern businessman, who is up-to-date in his view of business but traditional in his decorating taste. An Oriental rug atop wall-to-wall carpeting mixes old with new. Queen Anne chairs contrast attractively with the ultra-modern city below. And the overall cool and light feeling of the office provides a respite from the 100-degree temperatures outside.

The impressive and dignified character of this office comes from combining contemporary and traditional components. The single pedestal desk was custom designed and is bolted to the floor with a large steel plate under the carpet. The desk has a marble inlay top to project a dignified image. Light control is accomplished with dimmer switches and motorized drapery tracks.

Because the occupant of this 13x17-foot office deals primarily in spiritual counseling--he's a resident priest in a hospital--no work station is needed. Instead, a rosewood table is provided for conferences. Shelving for reference materials and for the closed-circuit TV is walnut. The carpeting is foam-backed for maximum noise control.

Dignified elegance was the goal of this office. The formal work area and informal conference area are set apart by color and the use of a fine Oriental rug over the carpeting. The glass-topped coffee table provides a large work area without obscuring the rug.

The office of the owner of a professional sports team has a strong design which offsets the effect of sports-related objects displayed in the wall unit. The suede couch is intended for informal business meetings. The shape of the area rug complements the ceiling configuration. A bold light fixture is as functional as it is attractive.

Walls

Most offices have four walls. Depending upon how lucky you are, one or two walls may be all or partly window. The remaining wall space is quite likely to be blank, dull, and possibly even painted a drab, institutional shade of green or beige.

Office walls are too often thought of as merely separations between one space and another. But you should consider putting walls to work to make your office different from, and better than, most offices you know. Walls can work for you in practical ways and can also help to project a particular atmosphere or character that can have an effect on you and your visitors.

Ignore the window area of your office for the moment and consider the remaining wall surfaces. Notice that all walls of a room do not have to be treated in the same way; in fact, treating four walls all alike—one paint color, for example—tends to emphasize the box-like character of a room. It is perfectly reasonable and often desirable to treat one wall differently than the other three or to treat adjacent or opposite pairs differently.

One different wall often develops naturally if one side of your office is a window or a glass partition. For practical reasons you may want to select one wall for special treatment, such as shelves or tack surface. In choosing one or two walls for special treatment, consider the shape of your office and the possibilities for giving an illusion of a changed and improved shape through different wall treatment. In general, stong, dark, and heavy colors and textures give an illusion of being close, while pale, soft, and cool colors and textures seem farther away than they actually are. Using these illusions can change a square and boxy space into a more pleasant seeming rectangle.

Even more useful is the possibility of making a space that is too long and narrow seem better proportioned. Try making the two end walls come toward you by using heavy and strong colors or materials on them, while making the side walls recede by using soft, light colors. The resulting illusion will be of a squarish, rather than elongated, room.

Another general point has to do with the sense of warmth in your office. If it now seems chilly and bleak—usually the result of north orientation and/or cool lighting—select warm colors and materials. If too much heat is a problem, from summer sunlight or excessive building heating, stay with neutral or cool colors. Check your color and material choices under the kind of lighting that will actually be in use, since various kinds of lighting can make colors look very different.

With these ideas in mind, consider the actual materials of your existing office walls or the materials to be selected if your office will be new. The most neutral of materials is plain plaster or plasterboard. Such bare walls are usually painted, and a new coat of paint in a better choice of color is one of the easiest ways to upgrade a dreary office. General advice about the use and significance of color given earlier applies here very strongly. Do not hesitate to use strong and unusual colors; refuse to accept complaints from painters or building managers that unusual colors are unavailable or too expensive. In the small areas involved in any single office, expense is no issue.

Only a few paint manufacturers make intense and lively colors. These are usually featured as "decorator colors" in better paint stores. Pick up color chips from one of these shops and insist on the color you want even if you have to buy the paint yourself. If you really want a wall of intense yellow, sharp violet, or deep brown, it can be obtained if you are determined enough.

Intense color may not be what you want at all, of course. White is one of the best of all colors, because spots of dirt or damage are easy to touch up. Avoid the sickly pastels that are favorites for residential decoration, and do not take the advice of a spouse, a secretary, or an "artistic" friend or relative too seriously, unless that person can show a record of highly successful color schemes. Magazines, catalogs, and books are full of color illustrations of both good and bad color schemes, and are a good source for ideas if you are uncertain about what colors to choose.

An alternative to paint for blank walls is some sort of wall covering. Wallpaper, an easy and popular wall treatment in residential use, often is too fussy and decorative for most offices. Where a feminine or fashion-oriented atmosphere is required, wallpaper might be a possibility—perhaps on just one wall. A number of the best textile firms offer wallpapers coordinated with their fabric prints, and these are usually of better design quality than the papers ordinarily offered for residential decorating.

The color and texture of wood can be had in wallpaper-like form in several products that use real wood veneer or simulated wood grain. These are available in rolls and are applied by a paper hanger just as wallpaper is. This material is not an imitation paneling, but an obvious surface treatment with a smooth and uniform texture. Look at the largest possible samples before making a selection and try to avoid the simulated wood grains that are obvious fakes. Another alternative wall covering is woven textile, which is paper-backed and applied like wall paper. Felt and velvet textures, as well as silks and brocades are possible wall coverings of this type. With a suitable choice of color and texture, this can be a very rich—and quite expensive—wall treatment, having hints of luxury and traditional elegance. Be very careful to select a highly skilled paper hanger, since installing fabric wall covering is tricky, and a poor job will look badly and will spoil an expensive effort.

A very popular alternative to all the above wall coverings is vinyl plastic sheeting. This material is very durable and can be washed or cleaned. The manufacturers of plastic wall coverings have developed an amazing variety of colors and textures, including almost every imaginable effect, both attractive and offensive. Solid colors with a slight texture, such as a stipple or a fine linen-like weave, are good alternatives to paint for large surfaces and are available in a great range of colors. Stronger textures, weaves, suedes, leather grains, grass-cloths, wood grains and even metallics are also very successful. Avoid the more garish patterns and imitative designs simulating improbable materials—marble or bamboo, for example. As with paint, remember that one wall, or two, in a particular color or texture can be better than all four painted the same color.

Almost as common as plaster or plasterboard are movable partitions made up of standard panels than can be taken apart and reassembled. The panels usually are made of metal and have a factory-applied paint or woodgrain finish. These systems are very practical where office layouts are changed from time to time, so they are great favorites in many institutional and corporate office groups. They tend, unfortunately, to exude a sense of stereotyped organizational bureaucracy and, with their green or gray color and expanses of glass, are responsible for the dreary grimness or many organizational office complexes.

If your office has metal or metal-and-glass partition system walls, they present quite a challenge to your ingenuity. Since the panels have very durable factory-applied, baked-on paint, it is usually unwise, and often even forbidden, to repaint them. Vinyl wall covering can be practical, especially if applied with an adhesive that permits later removal. Where some or all of the panels are glass, the problem is somewhat easier to deal with. Glass tends to appear cold, is sound-reflecting, and will limit your privacy while presenting you with an outward view that may be unattractive or distracting. If you need or enjoy the outward view, you will accept the glass as it is. But where it is not what you want, various means of partial obstruction are available.

Blinds, either vertical or horizontal, or drapes are possible choices for obstructing a bad view and can be used just as they would be at outside windows. Vertical Venetian blinds are probably best and come in many colors and textures. Patterned or textured glass can be installed in place of clear glass by any glazer; it cuts vision while permitting light to pass and is often intrinsically attractive. Gray or bronze colored glass or semi-mirror also is possible, but remember that the poor acoustical qualities of glass will remain and can only be escaped by changing glazed panels to solid ones with good acoustical characteristics.

There are also more informal ways of dealing with glass walls. For instance, you can place good-sized plants in strategic locations to block unwanted lines of sight or paste up (with transparent tape) temporary display materials— posters, recent brochures or advertisements, maps, charts or other such material. Choose carefully to avoid a sense of clutter, and remember that such material must look good from the outside as well as from the inside of your office. A small number of fairly small but attractive items used in this way can block vision in key directions and make a glass-partitioned office look active, lively, and interesting.

Paneling is one of the traditionally luxurious ways of treating fixed walls in an office. Traditional wood paneling is made up of a system of rails into which the panels are fitted. These panels can be in a natural wood or painted white

Large plants and temporary display materials such as posters can be used to increase privacy in glass-partitioned offices. They also can make the space look lively.

or some other light color. This kind of paneling involves skillful woodworking and is therefore expensive and something of a recognized status symbol. Do not trust an average carpenter to do a paneled wall or room. The design must be worked out carefully and must be expertly detailed. Attempts to simulate traditional paneling are sometimes made by covering a wall with plywood and nailing on surface moldings. This always looks artificial and pretentious.

Modern wood paneling does not use traditional moldings. Instead, large, unbroken areas run from floor to ceiling in narrow strips, planks or boards, or in sheets of plywood up to four feet wide. Joints may be smooth and flush, covered by a modern wood or metal molding, or treated with a groove or recess. The choice of wood color and finish is very wide and a single wall paneled in this way usually looks very good. Avoid cheap prefinished sheets available from lumber yards and intended for do-it-yourself home installation. These materials do not look like real paneling and give an office the character of a basement TV room.

Floor-to-ceiling and edge-to-edge mirror is a possibility, but it has a lot of negative points. It is a dramatic treatment and will, of course, double the seeming visual space of an office. But it is expensive and it also leaves you and anyone else in the office constantly confronting self-images that may become disconcerting. Reserve it for offices in fashion- or stage-related fields in which personal appearance and projection of self-image is of key importance.

Fabrics also can be stretched over wall material with good effect. Simply cover inexpensive wallboard, preferably a sound-absorbing type, with smoothly stretched fabric. The fabric is wrapped around the edges of the board, as you would wrap a package, before the panels are mounted on the walls. Joints show as neat, vertical seams. Such walls also make good tack surfaces since the material is "self-healing" to pushpin holes. On a smaller scale, you can obtain oil painting canvas stretchers from any art supply store and stretch an attractive textile, (a solid color or a simple pattern, such as stripes) over a lightweight backing. Staple the edges at the back just as an artist would staple a canvas. The unit is then hung just as a painting would be. This is an excellent way to deal with metal partitions, for example, and has the advantage of being easy to change or to move from room to room. This idea works best where the panel or panels are quite large. You may have to order the stretchers custom made, but the cost is very low in relation to the effect that is possible.

It is possible to use regular window drapery where there is no window at all. Often, this is done in a windowless office to suggest the presence of a window. It works best when special lighting is directed at the drapery to make it seem like a source of light, at least in psychological terms. Fake windows used in stage design are, of course, an absurdity and should not be attempted in any office.

You can also use various textile materials as wall

Many fabrics printed with beautiful designs are available at low prices. Canvas stretchers are easy to assemble. Fabric can also be stretched over wallboard for interesting results.

hangings. Tapestries and rugs are effective in this way, as are some modern craft weavings. Hanging a blanket or quilt, stretched between wood strips at top and bottom, also can look good. Be sure that the item hung is of fine quality, and display it as a work of art.

There are a number of practical uses for wall surface that can also be visually attractive. The most obvious is tackboard. Dark brown insulation cork usually looks best, but some standard tack boards now come in pleasant tones of tan or brown. The wall will look best if the tackable material covers it from edge to edge and from baseboard to ceiling. Once the tack surface is in place, it is up to you to choose attractive material to display and arrange well. Update the displayed material regularly so that your wall is not cluttered with old and faded material. Chalkboard is also available in blue, brown, and green, as well as the traditional black. If you like to sketch or calculate as you talk, a large chalkboard may be a very useful, as well as attractive, surface. Small framed tack boards or chalkboards usually look rather drab and unattractive. A magnetic metal surface is a compromise that permits pinning up material with small magnets as well as writing with crayon or grease pencil.

Another attractive and utilitarian wall treatment is book shelving or a combination "storage wall" that may include closets, bar, drawers, and shelves. Book shelving is fairly simple to build and install, which makes it fairly inexpensive. But, be sure that you really will have books and objects to fill the shelves. Books generally give a sense of thoughtful or learned activities and look good, too. Some objects, especially if they are related to your work, can look good on display, but avoid the kind of collection of decorative knick-knacks that often show up in home "room dividers." More elaborate storage units involve complicated, costly cabinet work and must be well designed. Several systems offered by furniture manufacturers can also be used to create a semi-custom storage wall made up from standard components. Maps, charts or plans can make an interesting wall surface if they relate to your work or interests in some way. A world, continent or area map with dots, pins or lines to mark significant routes, places or territories is often helpful as a conversation starter and is attractive as well. A wall display of products, packages, photographs or graphic materials is also a way to call visitors' attention to the specifics of your work. Business graphs and charts can work in the same way, but be sure that they are attractive and that they do not display confidential or troublesome data.

A well-planned bookshelf system is a wall treatment that can be as attractive as useful. Books nearly always look impressive.

Photomurals are also a possibility if your field generates suitable subject matter. A giant air photo of a landscape, or a blowup of micro-crystaline structure that can stimulate conversation about your work can be interesting and helpful. Using vague, pleasant outdoor scenes to make a space larger usually comes across as forced and inappropriate.

You might also consider the kind of wall treatment usually called "super-graphics," big abstract patterns in color and line that have no specific meaning but that liven up a space that would otherwise be uninteresting and colorless. Commission a good graphic designer to design super-graphics if you want to take this direction, and have the execution carefully supervised so that the result will be professional, neat and durable.

Windows

A natural human need for light and air and escape from claustrophobia makes the windowed office very desirable. If it is your good fortune to have one or more windows, you will want to consider how they should be treated for best possible function, appearance, and expression of character. Consider the windows you have in relation to the following checklist.

1. Is the view pleasant, indifferent, or unattractive? An unattractive view will require some thought to preserve the window amenity while screening the view.
2. Is the window light useful or, possibly, too strong — at least at certain times of day or seasons?
3. Is there a problem with cold and drafts in winter and/or hot sunlight in summer?
4. Is the appearance of the window (its frame, glazing, etc.) attractive, neutral, or unattractive?
5. Is the window well placed in its wall and in relation to the office as a whole? Some windows are off center, in a corner, at odd heights, or of strange shapes that will require some special treatment.
6. Where, in a range from businesslike and utilitarian at one extreme to frilly and decorative at the opposite, do you place your office? (Window treatment is very expressive in this range.)

The list of tools for attacking these problems is fairly short, including various kinds of drapery, blinds, shades, shutters, louvers, and screens used singly or in combination. Before making a choice among these alternatives, think about Question 5 above. If your window or windows are well placed, any window treatment may be suitable. In

Drapery can be used to conceal an oddly placed window and help an office achieve a look of symmetry. However, there's nothing inherently wrong with an off-center window.

modern interiors, there is nothing wrong with having a window opening off center if it is logically and attractively placed in relation to the general layout of the room. However, if the window or windows are oddly off center or of odd shapes and sizes, blinds or drapes can be used to conceal the oddity.

Drapes also can be used to deal with the window-related problems of radiators or convectors, which usually are centered below windows and often are unattractive. In the case of a single radiator unit, a cover or baffle can be installed to give the radiator a more clean-lined appearance. Floor-length drapes can then be installed to soften the lines of both the window and the radiator cover. The drapes, of course, would have to remain at least partially open when the radiator is functioning. Alternatively, a radiator cover can be installed to run from wall to wall. Wall-to-wall drapes can then be hung to extend down only to the top of the radiator cover. This is a good way to deal with multiple radiators and/or windows.

In many modern buildings, windows extend across an entire wall and even from ceiling to floor. If the view is good, this is a dramatic and attractive situation, but you probably will want some treatment to control excessive brightness of sunlight and to cover the glass area should you work at night or late on winter afternoons when the dark sheet of glass may seem cold and depressing. In many cases the building will provide window treatment, and may even *require* a standard window treatment to maintain a uniform external appearance. A common standard treatment is roller window shades of a standard color. In older buildings with small individual window openings, or in more modern buildings, venetian blinds or vertical blinds are often used instead of shades. It is possible that you will not require any further window treatment, but most often you will want some additional elements to give you more control over the amount and the quality of light and to soften and personalize the standard treatment. This may mean adding drapery inside the line of blinds or adding curtains or blinds at individual window openings.

It is possible, of course, to construct a false wall, having any sort of desired window openings, against the existing windows. But this is a very expensive process and likely to generate an artificial feeling. This is usually done when a tenant in a modern glass-walled building decides on a traditional interior; since it is hardly possible to have a Georgian colonial office with floor to ceiling glass, a false inner wall is built with small multipaned windows set into it. If one is determined on any such traditional effect, it is probably best to select office space with appropriate window openings rather than to resort to such stage-set decor.

In most cases, simple window treatments seem most appropriate in offices, while elaborate and traditional window drapery suggest residential uses. Pullback drapery, cafe curtains, prominent brass rods and rings, and similar fussy details are best avoided unless some special nostalgic or homelike atmosphere is required.

In many modern buildings, windows extend from floor to ceiling. An unattractive view or too much sunlight can be blocked with horizontal blinds--perhaps of the narrow-slat type.

Blinds

Roller blinds are inexpensive and practical but not usually very attractive. Better blinds can be made in handsome materials, including most available textiles. Consider a special installation in which the roller is hung by a special pulley

system at the bottom of the blind. This arrangement permits opening or covering any part of the window from top to bottom.

Roller blinds are most useful for individual window openings that are not too wide. Black-out blinds are available and useful if film or slide projection takes place in your office. They may be desired for that specific purpose even if other window treatment is provided.

Roman blinds pull up via a cord into neat accordian folds and are best suited to some traditional styles of decor.

Matchstick or slat blinds are made up of bamboo or wood strips and a cord pulls them up into rolls. These are very inexpensive (particularly some imported bamboo types) and can look very good, although they are somewhat informal in character. They can hang in the window opening or can be wider, extending across part or all of the room width.

Sun control and energy-saving blinds are available in a number of special materials. Plastic sheeting — tinted, reflective, or both — can be fixed in place or mounted as roller shades. New woven materials, such as "thermo shade" and "thermo veil" act as sun control louvers on a micro scale. Some highly sophisticated systems are coming into use in which automatic light or heat sensors activate motorized controls to adjust blinds to optimum settings to conserve heat in winter and minimize summer air conditioning loads.

Horizontal venetian blinds are probably the most widely used of all office window coverings and are universally familiar. Slats may be of wood or aluminum in a range of colors and metallics. You can even get a different color on each side of the slats. Venetian blinds can look somewhat routine and utilitarian — they must be kept clean and undamaged. It also takes some care to be sure that they are pulled to a consistent level, straight and with veins set at a consistent angle. When venetian blinds are used for light control, drapery can be added to soften the appearance of the total treatment. Slat width ranges from 2 inches to as narrow as 5/8 inch. Narrow-slat blinds look more modern and attractive to most viewers.

Vertical venetian blinds have become a very popular alternative to drapery and/or horizontal blinds. They can pull to the side and the louvers adjusted to control light and view. The veins can be of various materials and colors and are usually quite wide — 4 to 6 inches. The bottoms can hang free or can be held in a track. Floor-to-ceiling installa-

Vertical blinds also are often used instead of drapes and horizontal blinds to control the light and the view from a large window. They are available in many colors and materials.

tions are most common, although ceiling-to-sill height is also possible, particularly where there is a radiator or convector cover. Vertical blinds look very contemporary and handsome to most people and, so, have become a special favorite in today's office design.

Drapery

Drapery is the other widely used office window treatment, either alone or in combination with blinds. Office drapery is usually hung from a ceiling level track or traverse rod in a simple vertical hanging with sewn-and pinned-in pleats at the head. A very wide range of suitable textile materials are available in a great variety of weaves, colors, patterns, and prints. Most curtains are made with linings to stop light transmission, but sheers made of thin, translucent fabrics can be used unlined to permit light to pass through and show up the pattern of weave. Various kinds of netting are also suitable as drapery that will pass light. A double line of drapery is often used to provide a sheer near the window and a heavier, lined inner drapery to provide flexible control of light and appearance. Drapery can, of course, hang to the floor or only to sill height. Drapery contractors and most upholstery shops will measure for drapery, calculate the yardage required (be sure to allow ample "fullness," the excess width that makes curtains hang well when closed), and will work out details of hardware, weights to aid hanging, lining, etc. They will also take care of installation. Drapery requires cleaning at regular intervals and will eventually need replacement, although the life of good fabrics, well cared for, is quite long.

Drapery tends to introduce a feeling of softness and luxury into an office. The color and pattern can set emotional tone by suggesting gaiety or dignity, simplicity or richness, coolness or warmth, or any number of other qualities. Do not limit your shopping to textiles available in retail shops or suggested by a drapery contractor. Textile houses that specialize in quality drapery materials have showrooms in major cities. Many furniture companies also offer lines of textiles that include drapery fabrics of interesting and lively design.

Special Window Treatments

A special problem or a need for a special look, might suggest any of the following window treatments:
1. Shutters, large or small, plain or louvered.
2. Fabric stretched smoothly over a frame that is arranged to slide on track like a sliding door.
3. Shoji screen panels on sliding tracks (similar to the above but of specifically Japanese design character).

4. Multiple drapes or panels on tracks (as many as six to eight) permitting one treatment at a time to be visible while others are hidden, thereby allowing for quick changes of "scenery."
5. Metal chain, links or beads in strands that form a kind of curtain.

At the ceiling, it is possible to provide some treatment that will cover and hide the head of drapery or any view of raised blinds or shades. The two typical ways of doing this are with a valance or with a ceiling cove or pocket. A valance is a narrow panel that extends down from the ceiling or runs along window tops. The drapery track is installed behind the valance. A cove, or pocket, must be constructed when the ceiling is installed. It is a sort of channel recessed in the ceiling. The drapery track is installed in the cove and is thereby hidden from view. Decorative valances, often used over individual windows in residential situations, are not appropriate for office use. The exception is in traditionally styled offices where decorative valances are part of the overall character.

Drapery surfaces often look more attractive when specially lighted. Wall washers or strip "track lighting" can be directed at closed drapery to provide a source of soft, indirect bounce light coming from the direction of the window. Pockets or valances can be planned to incorporate strip lighting that will light a drapery area in a similar way.

There are also a few unusual window treatments in which the window itself is used as a kind of display area. The most familiar possiblity is use of the window for a display of plants — large plants or small trees on the floor, smaller plants at sill level, and plants hanging from the ceiling into the window space. Natural light will make plants grow well, and they become both screening and decoration. Shelves can be set up or hung in front of a window to provide display space for objects — most effectively transparent or translucent objects such as bottles or glassware. A display of this sort must relate in some way to the use of your office, or at least to some specific personal concern. A window display of perfume bottles might be an interesting and attractive element in your office if perfume and cosmetics are part of your business.

Windows and window treatments should be regularly cleaned, repaired, and otherwise maintained. Dirty curtains, or blinds that hang askew or are left always lowered even in good weather, are all too common in offices. Take a moment every day to adjust blinds and curtains as they should be.

Ceilings

Every office has some sort of ceiling, of course, and that might be the reason ceilings receive less thought and attention than perhaps any other aspect of office design. We are usually content with any ceiling that is not unattractive or offensive. In many older office and loft buildings, office space has no finished ceiling, so there is an overhead tangle of beams, air conditioning ducts, pipes, and dangling light fixtures. If the walls do not reach to the slab above, sound will carry from space to space. This reduces privacy and is annoying. Improvement in this situation involves stretching the walls all the way up to a solid surface and then adding within the enclosed office a "hung" or "suspended" ceiling.

In better and newer offices, a hung ceiling will usually already be installed. A new hung ceiling requires professional installation. It must meet building regulations and include provision for lighting, air conditioning, sprinkler heads, and usually some kind of acoustical treatment. Actually, a hung ceiling is often called an acoustical ceiling because the most usual surface is some type of acoustical tile or panel. A good-quality, older form of this type of ceiling makes use of plaster (or acoustical, sound-absorbing plaster) on metal lath. In offices of traditional design, a plaster ceiling is often edged with moldings of period design. If your office happens to have this kind of ceiling, it needs only to be kept painted. Modern hung ceilings use 1-foot-square acoustical tiles, or panels of acoustical material measuring 2 by 4 feet. The tiles or panels are held by metal T-bars or Z-bars so that they are easily installed without wet materials, and can be removed to give access to wiring and ducts above. The tiles and panels come in many designs

Modern hung ceilings made of acoustical tile can be used to conceal air conditioning ducts, wiring, beams, and pipes. They help to cut noise. Lighting panels (lighter areas, right) can be built in.

and are rated with an NRC value that tells how effective they are in absorbing noise. Tiles with many little holes and a beveled edge are cheap and effective, but can look crude and ugly. The best tiles have a texture with irregular fissures resembling travertine marble, and a flush edge. The

joints are hardly visible and the ceiling looks smooth and neat.

Larger panels are often installed with visible metal strips at the joints and are simply laid in place. This makes access for repairs easy. A modular sizing on a 2-foot-square or 2-by-4-foot grid is usual in order to match up with standard sizes of light fixtures. Air conditioning inlets can be grilles or, preferably, be concealed by being part of the light fixtures or support runners. There is also a wide variety of "integrated ceilings," in which acoustical surfaces and lighting and air conditioning systems are combined in some neat and attractive way, but are more visible and noticeable than the usual smooth surface. Manufacturers of ceiling systems offer elaborate literature on their products. These companies will arrange for professional installation. In most cases, a single private office can be best served by a simple, smooth ceiling that attracts no attention. White or off-white is the preferred color: The resulting light reflection is efficient and pleasant. If indirect lighting is used, a white ceiling is essential. Strong or dark ceiling colors are often used to de-emphasize overhead clutter where no hung ceilings exists, but are not generally desirable in offices. In a private office, the acoustic value of the ceiling is of little importance, especially if the floor is carpeted, since there will usually be little noise to absorb. Annoying sound such as that which comes through a thin partition wall or an open door is not diminished much by an acoustical ceiling, so there is little reason to worry about NRC ratings. This means that painting over an acoustical ceiling is all right, even though the paint might hurt the NRC rating of the material. These ratings mean much more in an open general office or typing pool where noise can be very disturbing.

Complex Ceilings

There are situations in which more complex ceiling treatments may be helpful. A few of them are:

1. A ceiling "cove," a slot around the edge of a central area of lowered ceiling with lighting concealed in the cove so that light floods the walls from a hidden source.
2. The reverse of a cove is "recessed" ceiling where the edge is lowered and a central area is a bit higher, with or without lighting where the ceiling level changes.

A coffered ceiling has a waffle-like look. A light source can be built into some or all of the squares.

3. A louver ceiling, either a commercial product or made up of venetian blind slats set in hung strips. This serves to conceal lighting and other clutter above while making access easy.
4. Luminous ceilings, a whole ceiling composed of a suspended translucent material with lighting located above it. These were very popular a few years ago, but seem to have lost popularity. This decline is probably due to the fact that the flat or corrugated plastic used for many installations tends to darken and accumulate dirt. Consider this type of ceiling only if your location is free of dirt and air pollutants.

A very handsome ceiling can be made of wooden flooring strips. Exotic and unusual woods can also be used. Recessed lighting fixtures are often built in.

5. A coffered ceiling, with many recessed panels — a kind of waffle surface— often with a light source in each square.
6. Stretch-fabric, usually white, installed with cords or threads tied so as to pull the material into unusual, tentlike forms. This is a possible route to a spectacular but low-cost ceiling treatment. However, it is probably too spectacular to be appropriate for most office situations.
7. A wood ceiling — regular hardwood flooring, for example, blind-nailed to concealed strips. More exotic and unusual woods are also possibilities. This makes for a handsome surface.

All such approaches will require professional help in installation and probably professional design help as well. And they tend to be anywhere from slightly expensive to very costly. Before exploring such complex ideas, be sure you have a clear purpose that will not be served as well or better by a simple and unobtrusive ceiling of a generally smooth white or off-white surface.

Lighting

Lighting is probably the least understood yet the most significant of all the elements that make up an office. Obviously, lighting has a practical, functional impact. Either you can see well or you cannot. If your office is less than ideal in this respect, you have a very real problem. Furthermore, the quality of lighting in your office is a key factor in the psychological ambience that your office projects. Is this a pleasant, warm, and responsive place or a cold, harsh, and seemingly mechanistic one?

Because lighting is usually built in, we tend to feel that it is not subject to change. It is true that built-in lighting usually requires a major upheaval to alter. But before you jump to the conclusion that nothing can be done on this front, take a few moments to analyze what the impact of lighting can be.

The lighting of your office influences your daily work experience in a direct way. But even though the lighting in your office is poor, you might not recognize this as a factor in the total experience of office life. As a result, you might not view it as an issue worthy of specific attention.

Standard office lighting is planned to provide sufficient brightness on the basis of standards that have been accepted in recent years. These standards call for a generous flood of light. There is a tendency to believe that this must surely be good lighting, since there is so *much* of it; in fact, too little light is not often a problem in a modern office. The human eye and brain are so adaptable that we can see well in a great range of circumstances, from the light of a candle up to the levels of full-noon outdoor sunlight. This is a range of about 5000 to 1. We recognize too little light as a problem only when the level of lighting is down to the most minimal, as in a telephone booth where there is almost no light for reading the directory.

While offering "enough" light (often two to four times more than necessary), modern office lighting sometimes does not address the issue of light quality. The most economical and, therefore, the most widely used type of office lighting is an array of fluorescent tubes in ceiling fixtures that form a pattern of bright rectangles in an otherwise dim ceiling surface. A light meter placed on a desk top will register an impressively high reading, but the daily experience of the office user may not be satisfactory. The lighting may be causing a daily negative experience that he finds hard to identify. If there is "enough" light, it is easy to ignore the buildup of irritation, exhaustion, and depression that can result from bad lighting. So, we shift the blame for these reactions elsewhere — to job tensions or to our own limitations, for instance — and ignore the burdens that inadequate lighting can put upon us.

These burdens are of two kinds. The first kind might be called functional, because it is a matter of less-than-ideal seeing. The second kind might be called psychological, because it is a matter of emotional impact that generates strain, even though the circumstances permit good seeing in the physiological sense.

The psychological impact of lighting is difficult to assess, and is a factor that can make your office work either for you or against you. Standard office lighting tends to be cold and harsh — "efficient" in the least attractive sense of the term. If you believe you must project an image of the cold, hard corporate VIP who is organizationally committed, this kind of lighting might serve you well. But it does not satisfy the needs of those who seek a more individualistic, warm, and personal expression of identity.

To test your situation in functional terms, check first for excessive brightness contrast. This term describes the situation in which there is plenty of light on the material that you need to see (the "task" in lighting engineers' terms), but there is also a very bright spot or spots that compete for attention with the task. It is vital that there not be anything in sight that is brighter than the focus of your attention — whether it is paper, another person's face, or a file cabinet. Many kinds of office lighting, by including overall light sources that are bright, defeat this objective. Most often the bright spots are the ceiling lights that are far brighter than anything else in the field of vision.

A second test relates to glare. Many of the things we need to see — print on paper, pencil notes on a pad, etc. — are to some extent glossy and will reflect glints of light from light sources. People twist the pages of a book or a sheet of paper, or move from side to side in an effort to solve this problem. The technical term for this condition "veiling reflection:" light that seems to cast a veil over the well-lighted object you are trying to see. The only equipment needed to search for this problem is a small mirror. Place it where a paper, book page, or keyboard will be. If you see the image of a bright light source, veiling reflections will be sure to occur. In general, the solution is to move the light, yourself, or move work so that the relationship between light, task, and eye no longer will reflect glare into your eyes.

To deal with the brightness contrast problem, consider any or all of the following steps.

1. If there are bright ceiling fixtures within your field of vision, a way must be found to block off their brightness. Traditionally, bookkeepers wore green eyeshades to deal with this problem, but that simple solution would now seem eccentric. A more feasible solution is to change the light fixtures to make use of low-brightness type fixtures, which are equipped with special louvers or lenses that make the fixtures appear dim from normal viewing angles while still delivering adequate light. These fixtures are a bit less efficient than the bright, glaring variety, but since more than enough light is almost always present, that is not a serious problem. However, such fixtures must be selected, ordered, installed by an electrician, and paid for — possibly too complex and expensive a chain of events. Sometimes it may be possible to change the lens or louver in an existing fixture.

   Another way to get rid of ceiling fixture glare is simply to turn those lights off. (This means setting up an alternative, of course.) Oddly enough, many modern offices do not provide separate switches for each office. However, the tubes can be removed from the fixtures and the lenses can be covered. If none of this seems practical, you can move your furniture so that the ceiling fixtures are not in your field of vision while you assume your normal working position. This is often not as difficult as it may seem at first.

2. Search out any other bright spots in your visual field and block or shade them. These might be decorative lamps or globes without adequate shading, or ceiling lights in an adjacent space visible through an open door or a glass partition. Change shades, use blinds or cut off these distractions in some similar way.

3. If you have the good fortune to have windows giving good light, consider relying on daylight as much as possible. This is energy-efficient and generally pleasant, but it requires a few modifications in most existing situations. There must be a back-up system for late winter afternoons, dark days, and night work, of course. It is also important to consider arranging furniture to make optimum use of daylight.

Daylight should come from your side: left if you are right-handed; right if left-handed. Light from the wrong side will generate a shadow of your hand when you write. A window directly behind you will force you to work in your own shadow. It also confronts visitors with a difficult situation in which you are silhouetted against the bright window. Some executives and managers have tried to use this situation deliberately as a gambit to enhance their power and dominance by putting visitors at a disadvantage. The visitor is well-lighted and easy for the executive to see, but he or she must squint against the light to see the executive's expression. Perhaps this situation might be helpful to an interrogator of criminal suspects, but it tends to block normal communicative relationships in most office situations. Light at your side will also be at the visitor's side, and you will both be able to see well enough for easy communication.

Using daylight also requires suitable window shading to control late afternoon sun and summer glare. Most office windows have some blinds or curtains. You may need better, more controllable shading if you expect to make full use of daylight, and you must be willing to adjust the blinds as lighting conditions change. Vertical louver blinds are probably the most useful of all light-control devices, and they usually look good, too. In fact, they can hide odd, ugly window shapes and sizes or block an unattractive view while still admitting light. Narrow-slat venetian blinds are also satisfactory, although they are more commonplace in appearance than vertical louver blinds. Drapery is not as readily adjustable as blinds and is therefore not ideal as a primary light-control device; it can be thought of as a secondary, more decorative item.

4. Check your visual field for very dark spots. (This is less likely to be a problem than overly bright spots.) Facing a black or nearly black wall or looking at papers on a black or dark desk top can also make the contrast between the task and your surroundings too great. Face a lighter wall or repaint; change to a desk with a lighter top or cover the top with a light-colored pad. A large desk pad is usually a good idea for any desk top that has a very dark finish.

Following these suggestions can eliminate brightness contrast problems, but your office may still have too little light, at least at some times of day. You must find ways to put back enough light to serve your needs without re-creating excessive brightness contrast or glare. If you have been able to convert to low-brightness ceiling fixtures, the following suggestions are only incidental ways to make minor improvements. But, if you have eliminated ceiling lighting, you must use some combination of these techniques (plus daylight, if available) to provide your primary lighting.

1. *Fluorescent lights.* Because of its high energy efficiency, this type of lighting remains an office favorite, in spite of the fact that most users find its quality and color somewhat cold and depressing. Fluorescent tubes come in a number of colors, and use of the slightly less efficient, warm-color types helps avoid the cold quality that makes people look harsh or sickly. In order of preference the available colors are:

> Daylight — bluish and unattractive
> Cool white — also cold for general use
> Deluxe cool white — utilitarian but acceptable
> White—utilitarian standard
> Warm white — better than white but tends to yellow skin color
> Deluxe warm white — most similar to incandescent, tending to warm skin color

With low-brightness fixtures and warm color tubes, the fluorescent light in your office may become quite acceptable. If you have given up on changing the ceiling lights and have turned them off, you might consider some new hanging fluorescent

Many different configurations of recessed incandescent lighting are available. These "downlights" can be installed to reduce glare while adequately lighting the task and the entire office.

110

fixtures that can be installed by an electrician without extensive changes in the existing ceiling. For some years, hanging fixtures were abandoned for use in well-designed offices because old-fashioned fixtures made offices look cluttered. Energy conservation moves, though, have reminded lighting designers that a given wattage provides more light the closer the source is positioned to the task it illuminates. A light six feet away from a task (in a ceiling, for example), moved to three feet away will give *four* times as much illumination (not twice as much as one might guess). This fact has stimulated the design of new hanging fixtures that are neat and attractive, highly efficient, and less likely than ceiling fixtures to be a source of excessive brightness.

2. *Incandescent lights.* These are the bulbs that are the standby of residential lighting. They are not energy-efficient, but when they are used to provide moderate light levels in small areas, this is not a big issue. Flush ceiling installations using "downlights" can be laid out to avoid glare, and standard lens or louver fixtures can control brightness contrast. Similar fixtures can also be surface-mounted with exposed "cans," projecting from the ceiling.

Special ceiling fixtures called "wall-washers" aim light at an angle to illuminate display areas or art works. Sometimes they simply flood a wall surface with light that bounces back into the room to provide a soft general illumination. These also can be recessed or surface-mounted. Installation requires an electrician; but, particularly with surface-mounted units, it can be done easily.

Track lighting is another way to introduce new incandescent light with great flexibility. A bar-like track is mounted on or near the ceiling. Movable lights (a great many kinds are available) can be clipped on wherever needed and be moved and turned as necessary. Lights can be added or removed as needs change. The track usually must be installed by an electrician, although some plug-in models are available. The lights can then be moved and changed by anyone.

Even without an electrician's help, you can introduce incandescent light in a number of ways. Lamps are the obvious first possibility. A table lamp or two as part of a seating group provides up-

Track lighting is very flexible. A bar-like track mounted on the ceiling and lights having two-way swivels allow the light to be directed to any portion of the walls and ceiling.

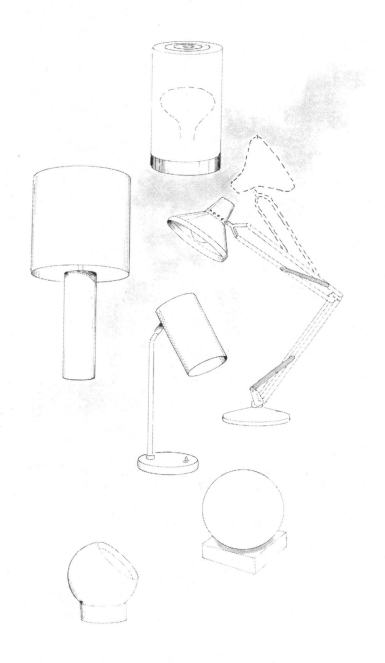

ward-directed light to provide general illumination as well as reading light in its immediate vicinity. Desk lamps are excellent task lights. Fancy decorative lamps are usually not appropriate for office use. Many simple and handsome lamp designs are available. However, it may take some searching to find what you need. Task lights can be an integral part of furniture ("work station" units are particularly suitable), or task lights can be separate devices clamped to a desk edge or supported on a base.

Hanging lights can be installed easily if they are plug-in types and have arrangements for running the wires back to a wall socket neatly. One approach involves using standard clip-on reflectors sold in photographic shops, directed up for general lighting and down for task lighting. If well chosen and carefully placed, this informal approach can work quite well. It is an ideal interim solution.

General light from incandescent sources can also come from "cans," which are similar to downlights. You stand these on the floor and direct them upward. Units of this type are readily available and simply plug in. They can be placed in a corner, behind furniture or in some unobtrusive location.

3. *High intensity discharge lights.* These are similar to fluorescent lighting in principle, but take the form of round globes, more like incandescents. They are very efficient and come in a range of color qualities. But HID lights are always high-output sources. They are finding increasing usefulness in large public spaces and are showing up in task-lit general offices to provide general illumination for hallways, lobbies, and other open spaces. In private offices, the HID lighting "kiosk," as it is often called, is a new kind of plug-in lighting device. A number of designs are available; a simple tube is most common. The light is directed up at the ceiling and bounces off to give strong general light in a large area. If you plan to try an HID unit of this kind, place it so that the ceiling area directly over it is not in your normal field of vision — otherwise, this may become a source of excessive brightness contrast. HID lights are slow in starting: they emit almost no light when first turned on and take about 10 minutes to work up to full output.

While thinking about good visibility conditions, you

should also think about what atmosphere you are establishing. This is not as easy a matter to organize as it might seem. We all can recognize the extremes of cold, harsh, institutional lighting and warm, cozy residential lighting. Neither is quite right for office life. We want the orderly, professional atmosphere that comes from good, even lighting. We also want an office that conveys a feeling of friendliness and pleasant dignity. Avoiding too much contrast and glare is a first step, but there is more you can do. Find out how you look to visitors in the normal light of your office. Ask someone to sit in your usual spot while you sit across from him. Are there ghastly shadows in the eye sockets? Does skin take on a green or purple cast?

Shielding overhead lights, avoiding too much cold fluorescent color, and introducing warm task lights can make dramatic improvements. Try temporary arrangements with lamps and clip-on reflectors to find better lighting arrangements. The best arrangement makes you and your visitors comfortable and allows you to look as warm and pleasant as you really are. Keep some basic stage lighting techniques in mind. Glare-free light, not too cold in color quality — which you need for good seeing conditions — will usually be pleasant light that makes you look your best. Light that is brighter at tasks than at secondary focal points (a conversation group or a display wall) will tend to be both energy-efficient and attractive. Separate on-off and dimmer switches on each type of light will also help you to set up ideal lighting for different situations and different times of day. It might be desirable, for example, to be able to open the day with blinds up, using full morning daylight alone. When a visitor arrives at mid-morning, lower the blinds, turn on task lights over the main desk, and direct dimmed wall washers toward a display wall. For an afternoon meeting, the blinds might be turned to admit daylight, and brighter incandescent light could be added over a conference or conversation group. An informal, end-of-day meeting suggests wall washers and stronger incandescents.

In every case, the aim should be to set the appropriate atmosphere for different situations: shirtsleeve business, a lively interview, a concentrated meeting, a relaxed conversation. All theatrical lighting is based on the idea that mood and emotional tone can be set, or at least enhanced, by the appropriate mix of color and pattern in lighting. Your office may not be quite so adaptable as a theater stage nor quite so emotionally volatile, but there is no reason you should not take advantage of such techniques.

Floors

Floors are easy to take for granted. We just get used to whatever is underfoot and never think about it. The floor of a room, however, is a large area that can set the tone of a space, for better or for worse. The other elements — walls, furniture, and the like — are tied together visually by the floors. Vision tends to sweep the area from eye level downward so that the floor is much more a part of our awareness, even if not always consciously, than is the ceiling, which is seen only when the head is tilted back deliberately. Also, the feel underfoot can transmit subtle psychological messages.

From a practical point of view, the floor surface is a big factor in the acoustical quality of a space. It is either a sound-reflecting or a sound-absorbing surface, depending on its material.

The floor takes wear, accumulates dirt, and must be cleaned and maintained with more care and effort than any other room element. Floors in a large office complex can be very costly; but, fortunately, the area in any one office is small, so even expensive flooring materials are probably affordable if the advantages they offer seem significant.

By far the most common floor in modern buildings is a grim concrete slab. A concrete floor can be painted, but painted concrete still looks drab and does not wear well; it is hardly suitable for an office. Usually a concrete floor will already be topped with one of the two most usual floor coverings. One is "resilient tile," made of asphalt, vinyl, or an asbestos compound. The other is carpeting. The former is commonly offered as a "building standard" in leased space and is provided without charge. Carpeting is becoming the favored alternative because of its acoustical value, its easy and inexpensive maintenance, and because it is generally felt to imply a higher status.

Older buildings very often have wood floors. They can be quite handsome and can be exposed or partially exposed if they are in reasonably good condition and are well finished. Soft woods (wide boards in old houses, for example) are much admired, but do not wear well. Hardwoods do wear well and were widely used in older office and loft buildings. Sanding down a battered existing floor will often expose a handsome surface that can be refinished with a modern synthetic varnish or lacquer (polyurethane wood finishes are ideal) to both look attractive and wear well. Old plank floors are sometimes painted in colors — even bright colors or patterns. This is an inexpensive treatment, but one that requires regular repainting as wear develops. An exposed wood floor is always somewhat noisy. It reflects noise and should be used only where other acoustical treatment (on ceiling or walls) is included, or where rugs will be used to lessen noise.

Resilient tiles laid over either wood or concrete are a familiar utilitarian standard. They wear well, and come in a great variety of colors and textures. They range from low to medium price. Resilient materials also come in sheet form (the familiar kitchen linoleum), but seams where the strips meet make sheet flooring undesirable for use in rooms wider than standard 72-inch roll widths. A good tile job requires a smooth undersurface, which is often plywood or hardboard over older wood flooring. The thickness of the tile, its material and quality, and the nature of the undersurface determine the appearance and "feel." Solid vinyl about 1/8-inch thick is both best and most expensive in the range of materials. Tile and sheet types are available in designs that stimulate such other materials as ceramic tile, marble, and wood. But the suggestion of cheapness that these imitations convey makes it wiser to choose simple textures or solid colors. Strong, solid colors are expensive. Many manufacturers simply do not offer them, since most users prefer patterns that help to hide dirt and damage. Cork and rubber tiles and sheets are also used occasionally. Tiles can be laid in patterns, such as checkerboards and stripes, with borders or inlays. Manufacturers' brochures illustrate many possibilities in varying degrees of good taste. Although practical in utility areas and in general office spaces, resilient tile in a private office suggests an austere and penny-pinching approach to decoration. It probably is not a wise choice unless

One alternative to very expensive carpeting is the use of rugs on top of an inexpensively carpeted floor. They are colorful, often wear well, and can be moved around the office easily.

you want to convey that kind of atmosphere. A tile of quiet color and texture may be a good choice as the basic flooring in a space where a rug or rugs will be used, but only a narrow strip should be visible.

Carpeting is becoming a nearly universal standard for offices that attempt any level of comfort and attractiveness. A wide variety of qualities, types of construction, color, and texture is available. The variety is so wide that it makes selecting suitable carpeting difficult. The confusing terminology and specifications used by different manufacturers does not make it any easier. Most carpeting intended for use in private offices is "broadloom"; that is, carpeting up to 12 feet in width, designed to reduce seams to a minimum. The older methods of carpet manufacture involved weaving the surface fibers into the backing with a firm lock. The terms Wilton, Axminster, and velvet refer to different kinds of woven construction. In recent years, tufted carpeting has become more common: the face fibers are pushed through the backing in individual tufts and are held in by a backing of rubbery adhesive. Sometimes the individual tufts pull out, but good tufted carpets wear adequately in normal use. Knitting and flocking are other kinds of carpet construction. Carpet pile can be "loop" or "cut," indicating the way the tops of the fibers are finished.

The basic fiber of the carpet pile is crucial to appearance and wear characteristics. Wool has been the traditional favorite for quality carpeting. But, because of its increasing price, it is being widely challenged by a range of synthetics. Most modern carpeting is made of synthetics, and only a few makers continue to make wool carpeting at all. Most designers and decorators are convinced that wool is vastly superior to any synthetic, but its current price rules it out for most large projects. However, in the small area of any one office, wool might prove to be the wisest choice. Wool offers a characteristic texture and look that synthetics cannot match, especially after a few years of wear. The way that wool wears and takes cleaning allows it to develop a kind of patina that is characteristic of many natural materials; synthetics simply break down and look unsightly long before they actually wear out.

Different manufacturers give different trade names to the same synthetic fibers. They also spin, twist, and mix fibers in varied ways. They claim to have found ways to equal wool, even though their products have not had time to be fully tested in use. The most widely used synthetics are acrylics, nylon, polyesters, and polypropylenes. Acrylics are probably most like wool in appearance and wear characteristics. Blends of fibers, and different ways of dyeing and making the weaving yarn allow for an endless variety of color, texture, and pattern combinations. Textures and patterns result from weaving or tufting, from printing color and pattern on the carpet surface, and from ingenious ways of cutting and modifying the surface of the pile.

The quality, feel, and wear characteristics of carpeting are also influenced by the underlay used (if any) and by the skill used in its installation.

Carpeting is now also offered in the form of "carpet tile" or "carpet modules." These squares can be laid down loosely or fixed to the floor with adhesive. Loose installation lets you pick up individual tiles for access to floor-mounted utility outlets. Also, the tiles can be replaced or relocated if wear or spotting takes place.

Carpeting can be ordered in special colors when large quantities are bought. A few suppliers will make up special patterns and designs to order. When ordering such carpeting, make sure you'll like what you are specifying. You will not be able to return the carpeting if you don't like it, and you will not have a chance to inspect a sample installation in advance. If the static shock produced when you touch a metal object bothers you, check into special carpets that have tiny metal fibers included in the material to "bleed off" the static.

Because of the complexity and confusion about kinds and qualities of carpeting, it is best to find a dealer with a good record of satisfied customers and to rely on his advice about quality and installation techniques.

If quality wool or the best of synthetic carpets seem too expensive, explore alternatives rather than settling for a cheap carpeting that will look substandard when new and will wear badly. Various kinds of woven rush, cocoa mat, and similar inexpensive fibers and weaves often look very attractive and are a better alternative to quality carpeting than bad carpeting is. Another alternative is to use a rug or rugs on top of a wood, tile or inexpensively carpeted floor. Rugs are available in an even greater variety of colors and patterns than carpeting, and they range from very inexpensive cotton and felt imports up to almost-priceless fine antique Orientals. Cheap rugs from India, Morocco, Mexico, or Greece wear well in relation to price, offer excellent choices of color and texture, and are easy to move or replace when necessary. Good Oriental rugs are available at moderate prices. The better Oriental rugs, though expensive, can be considered the most economical of floor coverings, since their value continually appreciates. But get expert advice before buying an expensive rug. Avoid machine-made "Oriental type" imitations.

If you plan to use rugs, consider installing a new wood floor as an under surface. A good wood floor can be left partially uncovered if a rug or two will be used at seating locations. The most handsome and luxurious of wood floors are laid with wide planks (approximately 6 inches) of hardwood such as oak, walnut or teak. Pegged attachments at the ends of the planks are a particularly elegant detail. Regular hardwood flooring of maple or birch is a less expensive alternative. Parquet flooring made of hardwood strips cut and laid in a pattern, most often a diagonal checkerboard with a straight border edging, is a traditional flooring of great richness. Modern parquet comes in prefinished squares that can be laid like tile in traditional patterns, or contemporary unbordered diagonal and straight checkerboard. Parquet should be of good quality. Some very thin factory-made tiles are likely to warp, crack, and make odd noises when walked on. The color of any wood floor can be changed by staining or bleaching. The final finish should be durable and not dangerously slippery.

A few other floor materials, not often used, should be mentioned. These are masonry materials, which are not popular in the United States, because they seem hard and cold. Still, they are durable and easy to clean, and can be very handsome. The sense of coldness and clatter can be offset by using an area rug or an inset of carpet in seating locations. Possible masonry materials include the following:

1. Brick, which can be laid flat or on edge, in line, in a checkerboard pattern or "bonded" as in a wall. Many colors and textures are available. The grouted joint lines can be colored to contrast or to harmonize.

2. Tile, which comes in a great range of sizes, shapes, colors, and qualities, ranging from tiny mosaic tiles to 6-, 8-, and 9-inch-square quarry tile. Tile in reds, grays or buffs is most usual, but glazed tiles come in a limitless choice of colors. They can be laid in varied patterns. Tile is particularly practical in warm climates, waterside locations, and wherever a tropical or Mediteranean flavor is appropriate.

3. Slate, in squares or slabs or more irregular flagstone, set in cement is another possibility little used. Flagstone gives a rustic appearance; squares and slabs can look formal. The characteristic colors are a range of grays from greenish to violet and from light to very dark.

4. Stone flooring is also a little-used possibility. Most

A new wood floor makes an excellent undersurface for rugs. A good one can be left partially uncovered if rugs will be used at seating locations. It is important to select good-quality flooring for this use. Some of the very thin factory-made tiles can warp and crack.

stones can be cut in thin slabs that can be laid like tile. Marbles in beautiful colors and patterns are very rich in appearance; they are popular in Italy and so provide a Mediterranean flavor. Granite, very durable and hard, is also a possible floor material. Colors run from rich browns to black.

The edging of floor material at doors and openings needs to be neatly handled, especially if the thickness of the material requires a slight change in level. Standard thresholds and edging strips are available for this purpose.

A final, practical issue is the wear that can occur where a desk chair is in regular use. Furniture legs and casters, and people's shoes scuffing the floor material all day, every day, will create wear in such areas while the balance of the floor remains in good condition. Tiles or masonry materials are practically immune to this problem. Wood may require refinishing every few years. But carpeting is a problem. Choosing a desk chair with the largest, widest and easiest rolling wheels made of a low-friction material will help. Moving the desk and chair a foot or two every few months will also help if there is room to do it. In the end, though, concentrated wear is inevitable. Special pads of clear or colored plastic are available, but they are unattractive and uncomfortable. Carpet tile or a carpet that permits an invisible repair is probably as close as anything to a solution. Be sure to make the repair before accumulated dirt and/or fading make the patch too visible. Regular vacuuming and cleaning to prevent build-up of dirt lengthens carpet life in any location. It must be accepted that carpeting will have to be replaced after a reasonable period of time. Budget for this and use the replacement time to make some color changes and upgrade your office generally.

Accessories

The small objects that are usually called accessories are the most personal, most easily changed, and often the most meaningful of all the components of an office. Every office contains a variety of ashtrays, desk pads, calendars, clocks, paperweights, pictures, and similar miscellany. The objects are sometimes useful; sometimes ornamental; sometimes neither. Even if organizational standards prevent your making changes in office walls, ceiling or furniture, you'll still have the freedom to change these smaller objects to serve your purposes to a maximum degree. Particularly in a standard office that is nearly identical with those next door, the small and personal objects become a focus of attention and project your personality.

Think for a moment about what these small odds and ends can be expected to do. Any or all of the following may apply to one or another accessory item.

1. *Practical usefulness.* In your regular work activities you may really *need* an ashtray, a clock, a letter tray or a paper organizer. But since you wear a watch, is a clock really necessary? Even if not, you may still want it for other reasons. Make up a list of accessory items you now have, consider additional items that might be helpful additions, and mark doubtful items with a question mark. Do you really use a pen from a desk pen set? How many paperweights does it take to weight your papers?

2. *Information for visitors.* Any visitor, particularly a first-time visitor, will scan your office, perhaps almost without thinking about it, yet picking up information about you from what is visible. A diploma or

license on the wall provides credentials that you might not mention in words. Family pictures give a clue to your personal life. A model of your yacht, a loving cup or a tennis racket suggest something about your sports interests. Your interest in the arts can be communicated by a painting. Think about the information you wish to give in this way and select it with care. A mounted game fish is an absurdity if you are not a fisherman; if you *are* an angler, a trophy that is too large and dominant may suggest that you are more interested in fishing than in your career.

3. *Conversation-making.* Starting a conversation with a visitor can be difficult or slow. Some informal talk about something other than the weather is a good beginning or a good ending for a meeting. Objects in your office suggest topics that may be useful to you. A travel poster may lead to a few words about your last vacation. An airplane model might give you a chance to reveal that you own and fly your own plane. A display of packages or products might give you a chance to tell more about your firm and your work. Such objects, which stimulate conversation that will be pleasant or give you a chance to provide favorable information, are helping you. On the other hand, you must consider removing objects that lead to boring conversation or to awkward or disadvantageous information. A degree that reveals you are only one year out of college and in your first job may not be helpful. Displaying honors and awards may make some visitors feel that you enjoy self-glorification.

4. *Work stimulation.* Pictures, models, products, posters, and advertisements that relate to your work — especially to active projects — will tend to stimulate your thinking and lead conversations to important topics. This is particularly true of creative work and promotional activities. Material of this kind must be kept up to date. A display of old advertisements may give information and stimulate conversation, but is less likely to encourage thinking about present and future projects.

5. *Your own pleasure and relaxation.* Objects that remind you of a pleasant vacation, your family, your boat, and other personal interests can generate pleasant thoughts and simply make you feel good in your

office. There is no reason to deny yourself this kind of comfort and support as long as you do not distract, disturb or bore your visitors in the process. A lack of this kind of personal material suggests that you are a cold "organization type" devoid of human warmth. Too much personal clutter may suggest that you are eccentric.

6. *Pleasure for visitors*. Entering your office should be a pleasant experience. This is the goal of office design in general, of course, but limitations of space and budget may mean that you cannot make your office a spectacular showpiece. Pleasant color in small objects can make an otherwise drab office look alive. Good art can be beautiful in its own right and provide a visual pleasure that routine work papers do not.

With your goals and purposes in mind, you are ready to set up your own accessory and art program in an orderly way.

Go over the things you now have in your office with a ruthlessly critical eye. Does it really help to have a brass nameplate on your desk? Is a cute snow-scene paperweight really meaningful? Are pictures of the company founder or the original plant or a framed first dollar earned truly helpful? Beware of anything that is coy, cute or comic. Such things may have anecdotal meaning to you, but are likely to seem silly to a visitor. If you really want to save certain souvenirs, treat them carefully and seriously. An old photo of the first shop or plant can be helpful if it is printed well and is handsomely but modestly matted, framed, and displayed. Collect the other accessories you need: ashtrays, clock, memo holder, etc. very slowly and carefully try to find things that are simple but beautiful and related in color, finish, and character to the rest of the setting you are assembling.

Objects that are genuinely old — not imitations — can help you convey a sense of tradition and of quality. They project nostalgia for the days of expansionist American business, perhaps, or the opening of the West and the building of the railroads. This may be an appropriate reference in some business contexts, but beware of setting up a stage on which the past takes the spotlight away from the present. Smaller old objects, such as a clock or wooden box, often look good in modern settings, but they should be of high quality.

Throw away any ugly or tasteless objects (gift-shop

items, cute souvenirs) that have no use, and search out suitable versions of the items you really want and need. Try to make such objects live up to your level (one hopes a high level) of taste and get rid of ugly calenders, meaningless tropies, and similar clutter. Family pictures are a tradition. Keep them small, neatly framed, and placed more for your attention than for your visitors'.

A clock can be useful and a pleasantly decorative object, but it has specific meaning in expressing your attitudes. Placed so that only you can see it, it is a strictly functional convenience. Placed so that a visitor can see it, it becomes a reminder that your time is valuable. The larger the clock and the more obvious its presence, the more clearly you will seem to be announcing your own sense of time and putting pressure on your visitor to be brief. You must decide how you want to express your own sense of this matter and choose a clock and clock position that properly conveys your intention.

A clock can be an attractive and useful accessory. It should blend in well with the overall design of the office. For example, a digital clock fits a modern office, a standard round clock goes well in an open office, and an elaborate wood period clock is suited to a traditional office.

Lamps can be detrimental. Many lamps are strikingly ugly and unsatisfactory as lighting devices. Matched pairs of lamps are particularly offensive since they suggest cute residential charm. Try to arrange lighting from invisible sources that will take care of practical needs. If a lighting device must be visible, try for something that will be functional and unobtrusive. Lamps made from vases, statues, jugs, or the like should be avoided.

Live plants — artificial plastic plants are out of the question — are positive, almost fool-proof elements. Even fairly large trees can be kept in an office situation, growing healthily, helping to maintain good air quality, and offering a sense of a warmth to everyone who notices their presence. The only mistake possible is excessive use. If plants prosper and take over so that the office turns into a jungle, they become distracting to the visitor. Plants are almost certainly perceived as "nice," but their role should remain incidental and supportive to the main function of the office, not dominant.

Hobby-related objects are sometimes a help in starting small-talk and in giving a visitor a better picture of your personality. Keep such things modest. A huge model of your boat, blue ribbons awarded your horses or dogs, and similar items might suggest that your hobbies are too important to you. Objects related to your work are better choices. A locomotive model is fine if you are employed by a railroad, but otherwise might suggest that you would prefer to be home running your HO model trains. A ship model

Live plants nearly always generate a sense of warmth. There are few ways to misuse plants in decorating an office. But it is possible to overuse them. Artificial plants should be avoided.

belongs in the office of a naval architect or a shipping official; a microscope in the office of a doctor or scientist.

Displays on walls or elsewhere have similar implications. A map or chart relating to your work, particularly if it is actually useful, is fine if it is handsome. Watch out for business charts that display the wrong information to the wrong person. Tack-board surfaces can be handy. Avoid the kind that are framed in metal or wood strips; an unframed wall area of dark cork or fabric-covered tack board is best. Choose what you tack up carefully and arrange it thoughtfully. A mess of old postcards, and yellowed memos and clippings have unfortunate implications. Displays of sports trophies is a cliché. (They might be appropriate in certain contexts, but more often are distracting and suggest that your mind is elsewhere.) You'll find that projecting your personality is difficult when you have to compete with a giant mounted swordfish or moose head behind you.

Art works — paintings, sculpture, and prints — are a means of making a space attractive and of revealing your taste and character. Be wary of poor art. It is usually better to display nothing at all than the kinds of hack work often offered in furniture stores or chosen by decorators to simply fill blank spaces. Some corporations develop fine collections of art works both as an investment and to help make their offices lively and attractive. If you can select from such a collection, you are fortunate. If you are really interested in art, you will want to study the kinds of things that will be suitable and that you can afford. Good works by known artists are very costly; works by historic figures are almost priceless. It is often possible to find good work by lesser artists, but beware of amateur art offered by relatives or co-workers. When in doubt, get an opinion from a respected gallery owner. Shun inferior galleries filled with worthless work at high prices.

Framed reproductions are a kind of fakery that tends to seem silly — everyone will know that it is not really van Gogh's *Sunflowers*. Prints and lithographs, even suitable posters that are well-mounted and framed, are better choices, since they do not pretend to be something they are not. Avoid pictures of cats and dogs, children with big eyes, paintings on velvet, and all such wares of gift shops. It is probably best not to display your children's elementary school art either, unless you can treat it like family pictures in a modest way.

Paintings and prints or other two-dimensional works are usually more appropriate for an office than is sculpture,

and tends to be more available in suitable formats; however, a small sculpture is also always a possibility. Select with care and only at a top-quality level. Avoid amateur work unless its quality has been confirmed by a serious critic whom you respect.

Art of good quality can be expensive, but first-rate work probably will appreciate in value, so it can be regarded as an investment. As with all collectibles, the best, which often is the most expensive, is most likely to appreciate. Even modestly priced prints or "multiples" by distinguished artists are likely to gain in value. Commercial "decoration" art or routine reproductions have no such possibilities.

If your work is connected with objects of any sort that are beautiful and interesting, by all means display examples, but display them well and keep them fresh and up to date. Shelves of books or magazines are ideal for people in publishing. Recent print ads of good design belong in an advertising office; record jackets and posters in media-oriented offices. Autographed photographs, in numbers, are a tradition in theater and film-related work (be careful not to feature one or two minor items of this kind all alone). In industry, manufactured products or parts of products under development or study are appropriate in engineering and plant-related offices, but at top management levels, they tend to suggest too much technical involvement.

Perhaps the happiest fact about the role of accessories, art, and small objects is that they are endlessly changeable. At a moment's notice you can take home, throw away, give away or send to the local thrift shop anything that is no longer an asset. Things that are new and current can fall into place as they come to hand and will help to make your office seem a dynamic and developing place — not a fixed and permanent setting in which everything always must remain as it always has been.

Design Professionals

If you have decided to look for help with all or part of your office design project, you will confront a bewildering variety of specialists who are eager to sell you their services. Sorting out these professionals and choosing the one that is best for your project can be confusing. In a rural location or in a smaller town there may not be many choices, but even in smaller cities you will probably find that there are: interior designers, interior decorators, office planners, architects, furniture dealers, and contractors; plus various kinds of consultants, manufacturers who offer planning services, and others who provide combinations of these kinds of services. Which of these services will prove right for you depends on the kind and size of the project you have in mind. It is worthwhile to consider each separately.

1. Interior designers (individuals or firms) are prepared to plan an office or group of offices and to select (with your approval) all of the furniture and other items to be purchased and all of the colors and finishes. They will make drawings for use by contractors, detail special cabinet work or other elements, deal with lighting, and help you find whatever contractors are needed to do the job. Depending on the individual designer, they will either do the purchasing for you, specify what is to be purchased or let you do the buying. In any case, you can expect to get the benefit of discounts that

manufacturers offer to designers and decorators. (An interior designer charges a fee that is separate from the actual cost of the project.)

Interior designers present you with plans and drawings, color charts, and perhaps even some realistic sketches or models so that you have a good idea of how your project will turn out. You can also expect a very accurate budget that estimates the cost of the project. If a project involves major construction work or filing plans with local building authorities, an interior designer may suggest that an architect be employed for this part of the job. Some architects work as interior designers too. And larger architecture firms often have a department that is really an interior design firm. For an office project, it is probably best to avoid designers who specialize in residential work. The professional term for office, commercial, and institutional work is "contract design."

2. Interior decorators (more often individuals than firms) usually focus their attention on the appearance of a space rather than on its planning and function, although some are competent planners as well. All decorators strive for aesthetic effect through choice of color, fabrics, furniture, and similar nonstructural elements that make up what is often called decor. If you want a traditional or period interior, select a decorator who is an expert in that style; other office design professionals might discourage period styling. A decorator will make sketches and, in many cases, color renderings. He will show you choices of color and materials in advance, as will a designer.

Some decorators charge a fee and handle purchases as designers do. Others insist on doing the purchasing and act as a kind of specialized retailer, using the decorators' discounts granted by manufacturers as their fee and billing you at retail price. This seems to make a decorator's services appear free, but in fact it may mean a very large fee. Decorators sometimes work for department or furniture stores and their services are then included in the price of the project elements. A package price for a complete room can sometimes be a basis for pricing a project handled by a decorator. To add to the confusion in the field, many decorators choose to use the title "interior designer." Since there are no restrictions on the use of either term, you'll have to ask many questions to discover which way a particular designer prefers to work.

3. Office planners, sometimes called space planners, are interior designers (sometimes an individual, but most often a firm) who specialize in offices and emphasize planning and layout. Larger firms are particularly well equipped to handle large office complexes—whole floors or multi-floor projects—in which organizational planning is a factor. Some office planners are interested in single or smaller group offices; others are not.

An office planner will generally work in exactly the same way as an interior designer. The only difference is that he or she is a specialist with greater experience in office work. This can be an advantage offset by a tendency to develop routine solutions applied to one project after another. Purchasing is handled as with an interior designer, and fees are kept separate from the cost of work or purchases, although the fee basis may be somewhat different. An office planner who practices in a particular city can be especially helpful in organizing contracts and supervising work as it progresses.

4. Architects are the most truly professional, since they must have a special technical education and a license (registration) that indicates they have met stiff standards and have passed a difficult exam. The architect's training prepares him to design buildings, and most architects concentrate on that kind of work. They are prepared to do renovations and interior work as well, if they are so inclined. Since every building has interiors, many architects develop a special interest in interior design and may include in their firms a specialist or a department devoted to interior work.

If your project involves construction work (adding a wing, changing structural elements) or requires filing plans, you will need an architect and may choose to give him the entire project, including the interior design aspects. If you turn over your project to an interior designer, he will tell you whether an architect is needed for part of the work and will select an appropriate person or firm for you. Architects are usually quite systematic about plans and specifications, and organize contracts and purchasing in a professional way. And a separate professional fee is always charged.

Recently, some architects have set up relationships with contractors or have begun to act as contractors on some projects. This is a new idea and still an unusual one. If you are considering such an arrangement, be sure that there is a very clear understanding about fees and professional responsibility.

5. Furniture dealers, office furniture shops and some department stores offer design services to their customers. At its best, the design service of an office furniture dealer can be equal to a professional interior design or office planning service. The difficulty is that, since the firm is also selling you its wares, you might always doubt the professional independence of the design service. They will inevitably choose the product lines that the store sells, whether or not these are best for you. And they have an interest in leading you to place a maximum order. In fact, the designer is often paid a commission on your order, and this gives him a motive to urge the most costly item for each situation. If you have a good idea of what you will be purchasing, using a store's design service may be a way to get some helpful, free advice in an otherwise do-it-yourself project. It is probably not wise to rely on a store's services for anything much more extensive than this. The store designer simply doesn't have the professional independence that you should be looking for.

Some furniture manufacturers offer a planning or design service also. Here again you give up the independent judgment of the professional. However, if you have already decided upon a particular manufacturers' product line, turning to this kind of planning service can be very helpful. The manufacturer has an interest in maximizing your order, of course, and you must be prepared to resist this tendency; but he also is interested in seeing his product used well, and will tend to provide helpful technical and planning consultation. This is also a kind of service that can be combined with do-it-yourself planning, or with limited professional assistance. Consider only the top manufacturers if you expect to rely on this type of assistance.

6. Contractors often offer design assistance. They might claim that there is no need for "expensive

plans," since they know what is needed from their direct experience. The contractor might offer "free" plans; and will "know a man" who can arrange for approvals, and clear away all bureaucratic delays. This is almost certainly a route to an ill-designed and bungled project. We're not saying that all contractors lack skill, knowledge, and experience; however, contractors are not designers, and so are almost certain to combine various design ideas that they have never fully understood. If what you require is *very* simple and clear-cut (moving a door, demolishing a wall), you may be able to rely on a good contractor to do the job without other direction. A good air-conditioning contractor may be able to solve a problem in his field without other supervision, but beware of leaving projects of higher complexity and scope in the hands of an unsupervised contractor.

Finding the right contractors, directing them through plans and specifications, and supervising their work are the most important roles played by the other office design professionals. A good contractor is a key to success in any project where construction is involved, but asking for design help from a contractor is asking the wrong source for the wrong thing.

In addition to the primary office project professional listed above, there are various specialists that can be helpful within their own particular areas of expertise. These include:

1. Engineers. Structural engineers are needed for major construction problems. For help with heating, plumbing, and air conditioning changes as well as major electrical changes, you need a mechanical engineer. An engineer can also file plans for building authority approval.

   Electrical engineers can also help with lighting problems, but often have a rather limited grasp of the aesthetic problems that lighting may involve. It is usually best to leave it to the primary design professional to decide if and when an engineering consultant is needed.

2. Lighting consultants are helpful for coaching engineer and designer to an ideal lighting plan. This aspect of design has become particularly sensitive with rising energy costs that make the cost of lighting a major consideration.

3. Acoustical consultants are often needed to help assure that the new office will have acceptable levels of speech privacy between spaces, along with acceptable minimal levels of noise. Sophisticated systems of background sound are now commonly used for arriving at a good acoustical environment, but expert consultation is important if these systems are under consideration.

4. Communication consultants are useful for planning telephone installations of any complexity. Now that privately owned telephone installations are a possibility, decisions about phone equipment have become more complex than ever.

5. Office systems and filing consultants can also be useful in larger projects. The planning of a new office establishes an ideal time to review paper-flow practices, and printed forms and filing procedures. Most filing turns out to be wastefully excessive with its tendency to provide for storage of a vast mass of duplicated and obsolete material. Microfilm and related techniques can save enormous amounts of space and major equipment costs. Other, more sophisticated, systems for information storage and retrieval through data processing terminals are available. Specialized consultation can help to determine what steps can best be taken on this front.

Selection of the right help for your project can be approached in a logical way by considering the following list of questions:

1. Are you planning to assign major project responsibility to a professional, or are you seeking minor, incidental help in a do-it-yourself project? In the latter case, define the help you need and seek the specialist that comes closest to offering what you need. A store or manufacturer's design service or a specialized consultant may be just what you require. You'll need to take some care in selecting a professional who will have a key role in helping you realize the office you need.

2. Will the project involve major construction or structural renovation? If so, an architect, preferably an architect with a special interest in interior design or office planning, is probably the best choice.

3. Will the project involve a large and complex space layout problem, but limited construction? If so, consider an office planner or "space planner."

4. Is this a problem in space layout, but with a further emphasis on space design in the sense of furniture, equipment, and decorative scheme selection? If so, an interior designer is a logical choice.

5. Are you making few or no changes in layout, but still interested in changing the visual appearance of the space? Either a designer or decorator might be appropriate, the latter is the obvious choice if you are considering period or other highly "styled" types of decoration.

In the end, whatever the person's title, your goal should be to find the person or firm that will be most attuned to your needs and best able to serve them with skill and efficiency. In choosing design help, it is useful to think over the following.

1. Do you need a large firm, a small firm or an individual consultant? A firm has a certain stability and continuity of group experience that can be reassuring, but a small project can be "lost" or delegated to a junior designer in a large organization. Individuals cannot offer the same stability, but often compensate for this with their intense level of concern for an individual project. You can always talk to your own individual designer, but may find it hard to get the top man in a larger organization to listen to you.

2. Do you need a firm or individual with a major "track record" in office design or can you take a chance on a less-experienced, younger person or firm? A track record offers reassurance and gives you a chance to see what sort of project is likely to result, but you may pay for the experience in higher charges and, possibly, a less-imaginative design. A newcomer to the field *may* do as well or better, but you should make every effort to make sure that this is the right designer for you.

3. How can you evaluate any firm or person you are considering? Ask to see previous work in pictures or, better, in actuality. Talk to previous clients. Anyone with a record of satisfied clients whose work you like should be considered. One disgruntled client from a past project may mean nothing, but a series is a warning. Education, membership in professional societies, publications, and similar credentials all can have some weight; but nothing equals actual projects and the experiences of past clients. The sense of personal rapport that you feel comes next. If you feel

ill-at-ease and doubtful, look elsewhere. If you are overwhelmed by a brilliant sales pitch, think twice. There are great design salesmen who disappear once a project is signed up and leave the work to less-qualified helpers. Ultimately, you will live with the project, not with the sales pitch.

4. What about fees? In the end, the designer's fee is less important than the job delivered and its total cost. Low fees are not a strong recommendation for a designer, but excessive fees are no recommendation either. This matter is quite complex and requires detailed discussion.

It is always wise, and entirely appropriate, to ask any professional about fees in advance of authorizing any work. Ask for some written communication—a proposal and acceptance is usual—that spells out the basis for charges before any work begins. Designers work on several different fee bases; sometimes one designer will use more than one approach for different projects. Commonly accepted fee systems are:

1. Time-based fees. This is probably the most professional of the approaches. An agreed-upon figure, per hour or per day, is billed on the basis of time expended as recorded on time sheets. The exact rate is a matter for negotiation, but in a firm there will usually be a scale setting different rates for the principal or partners and for each of several levels of staff. A monthly bill keeps the financial relationship up to date, and you have a chance to question, protest or quit after each bill arrives.

2. Time-based fee with fixed maximum. This is possible if the extent of the project can be spelled out clearly. The designer estimates the time that will be required and agrees not to exceed the resulting figure unless changes are made in the scope of the project.

3. Percentage of cost of the work. This is the traditional basis for an architect's fee, with usual percentage falling in a certain range. The range is usually 10 percent to 25 percent with 15 percent a typical average for interior design and renovation work. This is a logical basis for building projects, but for office planning it is often not completely logical. Parts of the project may be provided by the building management without charge, or you may plan to re-use existing furniture or equipment. This method also

gives the designer a financial stake in suggesting expensive alternatives over cheaper ones. These problems make this a less-than-ideal fee basis for most office projects.

4. Area-based fee plus service charge. Such a fee structure is often used by office planners. In this arrangement, planning is sold on a basis of a fixed cost per square foot. A typical range is $1.00 to $3.00. In addition, there is a service charge—usually 10 percent to 15 percent on all purchases of items selected or specified by the planner. This arrangement incorporates some of the better features of each of the other methods. However, it suggests a low fee at the time of signing (the modest fee per foot) and then generates a high fee as the service percentage charges accumulate. Some designers will also charge a special fee, as high as 25 percent, for designing custom-detailed cabinet work or special furniture.

5. Retail. This describes the decorator's practice of charging full retail price for everything purchased, while taking a fee in the form of the discounts suppliers offer to designers and decorators. This might sound like a free design service (and is sometimes called this by stores that offer decorating services), but can actually result in a high fee. The usual discounts range from 25 percent to 40 percent off retail list prices. There is, of course, nothing unethical about this basis if both parties understand it clearly and accept it as appropriate.

Consultants usually expect to bill for a fee on an hourly basis at an agreed rate. Contractors may be willing to bid at a fixed figure; but increasingly, contractors who do not have to search for work and who are beset with increasing costs are unwilling to bid on jobs. Instead, they prefer a "cost-plus" basis, according to which they bill for workers' time and materials at their cost and then add their overhead and profit as a percentage—typically 10 percent plus 10 percent or 15 percent plus 15 percent. Since this makes the cost of the work open-ended, you should ask for an estimate—possibly an estimate that is guaranteed not to be exceeded. Guaranteed estimates are increasingly difficult to secure from contractors and are often meaningless anyway, since every project involves changes and adjustments that are outside the estimated figure. Cost-plus is a satisfactory basis for working with a contractor who has a reputation for fair and honest charges on previous jobs.

High fees and excessive charges from contractors are often at least in part the fault of the client. You can keep expenses down if you are clear about your needs, specific in stating what you want, and prompt in making decisions. Endless revisions, changes in mind, and uncertainty about what is needed and what is not will result in gradually increasing charges that may become truly overwhelming. The client who finds the right designer, and gives clear instructions and prompt approvals will not usually have to struggle with excessive fees.

Office projects often involve one other specialist who is not, strictly speaking, a design professional. This is the real estate broker. If you are renting space in an existing or new building, your broker will help you to find the space you need at an acceptable rental. He is also the middleman in the negotiation between tenant and landlord concerning those improvements the building management will provide. An office lease is usually based on a rental per square foot, per year. The figure quoted will be on "rentable" space rather than "net" or actual space. This is because it is customary to quote rents on a basis that includes a share of public spaces, thicknesses of walls, and areas blocked by columns. Do not be surprised if the actual area you rent is 10 percent smaller than the rentable area you pay for. In addition, a "work-letter" is added to the lease, spelling out improvements the landlord will provide in your space— partitions, lighting, an acoustical ceiling, floor covering, and air conditioning among them. These items are usually included in rent at a quality level called "building standard." If you want more, or different improvements, you can expect to pay a premium on your rent or extras to the contractors who prepare the space. The poor quality of most "building standards" is notorious, and you can become a captive of the contractor who demands endless extras for every item above this standard. It is often best to rent space as is without improvements and pay the entire cost of work yourself. But you will then have to finance the work at the time that it is done. Your real estate broker, if he is truly representing your interests fairly rather than those of the landlord, will be an ideal advisor and negotiator in this complex and difficult scene.

Some real estate agents offer some preliminary planning help to assist in selecting suitable office space, often through an arrangement with a particular office planner. This can be helpful, but beware of becoming a captive client to a planner who might not be your first choice.

The world of real estate and contracting is, unfortunately, riddled with questionable and downright dishonest practices. This is especially true in some major cities. Kickbacks and payoffs are common; they often seem at first to be the only way, or the cheapest way, to get results promptly and easily. It is best to avoid such "deals" and to stay away from agents, design firms, and contractors whose reputation is uncertain in these matters. If you make it clear to everyone involved from the start that you will not tolerate any questionable dealings, you will find it possible to seek out honest people and organizations every step of the way. In the end it is the least expensive course of action and the only one that makes all dealings professional and pleasant.

Buyers Guide

An office can include a surprising variety of products, from a surprising number of manufacturers. The New York telephone directory lists 102 manufacturers of office furniture, and it is obvious that many names are missing. It should be understood that the Buyers Guide that follows is not in any way complete. It lists some brands in each field that represent a range of products and price levels. Every source that appears here has an established reputation and can be counted on for good value in its own class. Names not on this list may offer products of equal quality and may be able to suit a special need of yours better than a listed firm. This Guide will provide a starting point, however, and supply the names of a few firms to contact if you are seeking new sources.

Office products are distributed in several different ways that may seem confusing at first, but which are entirely logical. Materials that must be installed by a building contractor — such as bricks and tiles, paneling, and ceiling systems — are usually obtained by the contractor and priced together with installation in a total figure. Thus you can select and specify the material to be used, but you must give this information to the contractor when you ask for his estimate. You might not care what brand of material is used (paint or plywood, for example) and choose to leave the selection to the contractor. When price is a factor, you may want to contact the manufacturer. But he will give you only an idea of *relative* price; a specific figure will be given only to a contractor. A good contractor should be willing to discuss approximate costs of various materials and treatments so that you can take price into account. Having specified a material, beware of a contractor's suggestions that an alternative will be "just as good." He might be right, but he might also be trying to increase his profit by substituting a cheaper and inferior material.

Where you are using a material or treatment that involves installation, the manufacturer may be willing to quote you on estimated product-plus-installation cost and refer you to a firm for the installation. Carpeting is commonly priced this way. An electrician can give a price based either on his buying the fixtures or on your buying the fixtures. If you buy them, be sure to discuss with the electrician any problems that might arise from legal or union restrictions in your area.

A drapery installer (often also an upholsterer) will give a figure for making and hanging drapery, including hard-

ware, and will figure the yardage you need to order. He should also look at a sample of the material you've chosen to comment on its quality and suitability. Prices on blinds and shades will be quoted in a similar manner.

Furniture, lamps, and accessories — which do not require a contractor's installation — can be bought from retail sources (such as an office furniture store) at a posted price. Products sold in this regular retail way sometimes are of lower price and quality, and often of indifferent design; the manufacturers of better products have found that designers, decorators, and architects are the primary markets for their products, since these professionals are often decision-makers in larger office-planning projects. Manufacturers of the latter kind of products operate showrooms in major cities primarily for the use of design professionals. Any interested party may visit these showrooms, but cannot obtain price quotations or place orders. "List prices" may be available, but these figures include a large markup to accommodate professionals who charge on a "retail" basis, using the manufacturer's discount to obtain their fee. If you find a suitable product in this type of showroom, ask the manufacturer to suggest a dealer near you who can order the item for you. The dealer will quote you a price that includes shipping, delivery, installation, and any service that may be required. He will base his price on his cost for the item, the amount of service involved, the size of the order, and the amount of business you bring to him. The quote will range from list price to a figure of 33 percent to 40 percent less than list. Discounts are small on single items and small items but are larger if a quantity order for chairs or files, for example, can be placed.

Better furniture is usually available in a variety of finishes and upholstery, factors which also affect price. Orders for coverings made from the customer's own material (from a source other than the manufacturer of the furniture) can lead to extra charges and possibilities for confusion, error, and delay. Nevertheless, this is often the only route to something unique, which might be exactly what you want and worth the extra cost.

Traditional furniture of very high quality (Baker Furniture Co., Contract Division) is available in a variety of finishes and upholstery--factors that can significantly affect price. The extra cost is worthwhile if something unique is desired.

The services of a reliable dealer who has an established reputation to maintain can be very helpful. He can pressure a manufacturer for prompt delivery (12 to 16 weeks is normal) and deal with damaged goods and similar problems. Shipping damage affects about 10 percent of all furniture that reaches buyers, so be prepared for such annoyances. Installation may not seem an important factor

147

when you're buying a desk or chair, but uncrating, cleaning up, adjusting leveling glides, and making sure that the drawers fit and work are chores that someone must do. Working regularly with one dealer is best because you can secure his loyalty. But this is not always possible, since the dealer may not represent manufacturers of all the products you have selected. Some dealers can offer helpful advice and suggestions, but beware of pressure to choose a particular item or line: the motive might be extra profit rather than your satisfaction.

Furniture

The makers of office furniture, numerous as they are, fall into a few clearly defined categories. First, there are the makers of quality steel office furniture. Steelcase, Inc., is the largest (sort of a General Motors of office furniture). It has an extensive product line, a reputation for quality and reliability, and a generally good level of design quality. Similar product lines are offered by GF Business Equipment, Inc.; All-Steel, Inc.; The Shaw-Walker Co.; and perhaps a dozen other manufacturers.

A second group of manufacturers have built their reputations on superior designs generated by prominent designers. The leaders are Knoll International (Mies Van der Rohe, Saarinen, and Bertoia) and Herman Miller, Inc. (Nelson, Eames, and Robert Propst). These two companies form an elite in terms of design and product quality and deserve special attention. They are followed in our list by a number of lesser design-oriented firms that manufacture products sometimes of equal quality, but take a lesser role in design leadership. They are Thonet; Harvey Probber Associates; Brickel Associates, Inc.; and Zographos Designs.

A third group comprises the importers of top-quality design furniture. The leaders are Stendig International, Atelier International, Ltd., and ICF (International Contract Furnishings, Inc.). Imports are no longer the bargains they were a few years ago, but unusual design and high quality are still characteristic of these products.

Each of these sources offers a wide range of office products: desks, office "systems" furniture, and related seating. Most furniture companies also offer lines of upholstery textiles, and, in some cases (Knoll and Herman Miller, for example), drapery fabrics also. In addition, many furniture companies also provide some accessories and incidentals, plus task lighting integrated into the furniture. Traditional

Side chair from Steelcase (upper right), Tycoon chair from Thayer Coggin Institutional (upper far right), Eero Saarinen-designed chair and table (below right) from Knoll International.

Plastic table and chair designed by Vico Magistretti and sold by Castelli Furniture (upper left); desk and credenza designed by Chadwick, available from Herman Miller (lower left); upholstered panel wall system incorporating task lighting from JG Furniture (above).

designs are a specialty with Baker Furniture Company and Kittinger Company. They offer products that are excellent in terms of design and craftsmanship.

Cost of office furniture spans a wide range. Low-cost products are not necessarily of inferior quality; perhaps different only in character and style.

Some idea of price ranges for budgeting can be obtained from this chart.

Item	Economy	Average	High Quality
Desk	$300-350	$700-800	$800-3000
Credenza or side unit	200-300	400-600	500-2000
Desk chair	120-180	150-300	250-500
Side chair	50-150	160	200-250
Small conf. table	120-200	200-300	300-800
Sofa (two-three seats)	200-350	500-700	700-2000
Storage wall units (per running ft.)	80-100	100-180	180-300

Files

Files are offered by the major makers of steel furniture (such as Steelcase and GF), and also by specialized firms such as Supreme Equipment & Systems and Oxford Pendaflex Corporation. Files are expensive, so you should make every effort to study your storage needs to keep down your need for file cabinets. Typical costs:

Item	Economy	Average	High Quality
two drawer	$50-80	$80-100	$100-150
four drawer	80-120	120-200	180-300
two drawer, wood finish	80-200	120-250	250-500

Oxford Lateral Cabinet filing systems from Oxford Pendaflex Corp., one of many manufacturers of files.

Textiles, Leather, and Vinyl

In addition to the furniture manufacturers, explore specialized textile houses oriented toward the designer-decorator markets for your office fabrics. Small, 3-inch-square swatches are usually available on request. Large samples, called "memo squares," are full yard pieces that can be borrowed or purchased with permission to return for credit. Outstanding sources include Boris Kroll Fabrics, Inc.; Jack Lenor Larsen, Inc.; and Isabel Scott Fabrics. Scalamandre Wallpaper and F. Schumacher & Co. offer both contemporary and traditional fabrics. Many fabric houses also have lines of coordinated wallpapers. In addition, some offer leathers and simulated leathers for upholstery. Fabrics are priced by the yard, but widths vary. Be sure that the yardage you order will be sufficient for your needs. Ordering upholstery fabric from the maker of the furniture to be upholstered avoids mix-ups but may limit selection. Do not hesitate to insist on a special fabric if it will suit you best. Typical costs:

	Economy	Average	Top Quality
Per Yard	$6-20	$16-30	$25-150

Leather has a unique combination of feel and smell that conveys quality and luxury. Upholstery leathers and suedes wear well and tend to age gracefully, even as signs of wear begin to show. Vinyls and other simulated leathers are more economical and wear well also, but do not develop leather's characteristic patina. Leather does not come by the yard but by the hide, each hide the size and shape of the animal from which it came. Vinyls and other simulated leathers are yard-goods, like textiles. Leather and vinyl tend to feel hot and sticky in warm, damp situations. If you are uncertain of the effectiveness of the air conditioning in your office, avoid them; use another material on your desk chair; or insist on a "breathable" vinyl, which has a special texture and tiny perforations that provide air circulation. A wide range of beautiful colors and textures of leather and vinyl is available. The leather required for a particular piece of upholstered furniture will be shown in square feet — translatable into hides by the supplier, who can tell the square footage per hide of a particular leather. Since leather is more difficult to cut and sew than textiles, the cost of upholstery work is usually higher for leather goods.

Leather-upholstered Eames chair, available from Herman Miller.

Typical costs:

Vinyl	$10-25	per yard (54″ width)
Leather and suede	5-25	per sq. ft.

Carpet and Rugs

Carpeting is an especially difficult product to evaluate and buy because of the great variety of weaves, constructions, and fibers — each having its own claim to excellence. Wool has an outstanding record for durability and an appearance of quality that only the best synthetics can claim to approximate. Only a handful of manufacturers still make wool carpeting, however, and it has become very expensive. Avoid inexpensive carpeting developed for residential use, and avoid any carpet with a hard, shiny glint to its surface. A soft appearance, pleasant texture, and "feel of quality" in a small sample is a fair index of high quality and durability.

Carpet squares from Heuga U.S.A. (upper right), wool custom-design rug from Edward Fields (upper far right), and floral-pattern Oriental rug from Couristan (below right).

154

Typical costs (installed):

Synthetic Fibers	$12-24 per square yard
Wool	28-60 per square yard

Simple "ethnic" rugs are still often excellent bargains, and fine, expensive Oriental rugs are likely to be good investments. Materials such as rush and cocoa mat are good economy alternatives to carpeting and rugs. If you plan to use quality rugs, be sure to deal with an established dealer who has a good reputation. Remember that a 9-by-12-foot rug equals 12 yards of carpeting, so evaluate any price quoted in this context.

Resilient Flooring

These are familiar and straightforward materials, which present no special problems to the purchaser. Some points to consider are: (1) a quality underfloor should be provided; (2) heavy weights (greater thicknesses) are generally worth their cost; and (3) solid vinyl wears best, looks best, and is usually most expensive. Budget 50 cents to $4 per square foot.

Other Flooring

Alternative materials include hardwood, brick, marble, slate, stone, and ceramic tile. (Many of these will probably require one or more area rugs on top to limit noise and the sense of harshness.) Installation is as much a cost factor as the original material, so a contractor's estimate is the only valid indication of cost. A range of $1 to $20 per square foot is usual.

Partition Systems

A number of manufacturers offer systems of panels and frames that form convertible walls. Such systems used to be a favorite way of dividing up space in office buildings. But their use has declined because moving them is troublesome and costly. It usually requires repair of floors and ceilings and changes in lighting and air conditioning. As a result, such partitions are rarely moved. The best-looking systems can cost more than drywall construction, which has a superior appearance.

Wall Coverings

Paint is the most economical wall treatment and can be very satisfactory in appearance when a professional job is done on a well-prepared wall surface. There are innumerable manufacturers of paints of excellent quality, so the choice of brand is often left to the painter, who tends to choose quality paint because it makes his job easier. A good variety of ready-mixed or custom-mixed colors is sometimes difficult to find. Brands listed in these pages are reliable and offer "color systems" including a wide range of strong colors.

Wallpaper is seldom used in offices, although some suitable papers are offered by the suppliers of modern textiles. Fabric wall covering can be very elegant, but the cost of the yardage of textile plus workmanship will be high: expect to pay $10 to $20 per square foot. Vinyl wall covering is very popular because it covers minor faults in the wall surface, is easy to maintain, and resists minor damage. It also comes in a vast variety of colors and textures, including suedes and velvets that simulate expensive textiles quite effectively. The price range is also wide: $1 to $5 per square foot is typical.

Traditional wood paneling is a very handsome wall treatment but has become very expensive: as much as $100 to $200 per *lineal* foot is not unusual. It must be custom made and be installed by an architectural woodworking or cabinet shop. Ready-made plywood paneling is less expensive, but offers less choice in design and finish and lacks the quality look of conventional paneling. Prices usually range from $1 to $5 per square foot.

Plastic laminates also can be used on walls. These hard plastic sheet materials are familiar as the typical covering for residential kitchen counters and for cafeteria tables. They are also used as a more durable alternative to wood in many types of office furniture. For wall surfacing or for custom-made counters or shelves, you can choose from a good range of colors and patterns — including imitation, but convincing, wood grains. Cutting and mounting laminate is not easy — these require professional skills. The material itself will run $1 to $2 per square foot, and installation cost will vary with the intricacy of the job. On the average, allow about as much for workmanship as for the material itself.

Wood paneling, though expensive, is often desirable because it looks so attractive. One of the companies that manufacture such wall treatments is Forms+Surfaces. Shown is the bonded Hardwood system.

159

Ceilings

A suspended ceiling of one of the better acoustical materials costs between $1 and $3 per square foot. The "integrated" systems, such as those offered by Armstrong Cork Company, incorporate lighting and air conditioning and require specialized installation work. Only a contractor's estimate on a particular job can give a reasonably accurate idea of cost. But, unfortunately, a small project, such as one private office, will be more costly per square foot than a larger project. New acoustical material applied directly on an existing ceiling is inexpensive — 50 cents to $2 per square foot.

Window Treatment

In addition to drapes, a variety of shades and blinds are available in a very wide price range. Ready-made blinds of acceptable quality begin at about $1 per square foot and range up to $10 per square foot, according to the materials and the system of hanging. Vertical louver blinds are particularly satisfactory for office use. They are available in many materials and colors, including metallic, reflecting surfaces with energy-saving advantages.

Narrow-slat blinds from Levolor (below), Synercon 60 ceiling system from Armstrong (right) includes lighting fixtures, acoustical board, and ventilation equipment.

Specialized Products

Storage systems include special rolling units that permit mass storage in minimal space.

Screens or acoustical panels are part of the systems offered for open, or landscape planning by furniture manufacturers, and they are also produced by a number of specialty manufacturers. They are probably of interest only if you are considering an "open office."

Signs and lettering are available in standard systems that make it easy to replace the messy and amateurish taped signs often seen in offices.

Folding walls or other easily opened wall panel materials are sometimes needed where an office must be combined with an adjacent space from time to time. The perfect folding wall has yet to be invented; most available products present appearance or acoustical problems. The Modernfold door is best-known and works well.

Kitchenette units, similar to those used in small apartments, are often provided in offices to act as a bar or service center for a "lunch-in." Standard units are neat and practical, but require installation by a contractor, who must handle plumbing and electrical work. The unit will cost $350 to $600, but installation and enclosure can add that much or more.

Planum Inc. storage wall system manufactured in West Germany and sold in the United States by Richard J. Racana Jr. & Associates (below). Can lighting system from George Kovacs Lighting and track lighting system from Lightolier (opposite).

Lighting

Architectural lighting refers to elements that are mounted in or on the ceiling, or in other permanent locations. There is a very large number of manufacturers; most produce utility units and compete on a basis of price rather than quality. A small number of firms we've listed are known for better fixtures, including those with "low brightness" lenses or louvers. Prices vary greatly, since types vary widely and installation cost is a large factor. A downlight (incandescent) costs from $50 to $100 installed; 2-by-4-foot flourescent fixture costs from $50 to $200. A small project will be more expensive per fixture than a large installation that will be done all at once. It is a mistake to search out low-cost fixtures, since in a small space the total cost of fixtures will be low and the cost of installation will be the same, regardless of the purchase price of the product. Be sure that fixtures selected are acceptable under local legal and union regulations.

Lamps are separate lighting units that plug into a socket. A wide variety of lamps are available at retail, but most lamp stores carry decorative products designed for residential use only and are not suitable in most offices. Some office furniture dealers do a bit better, but the best lamps come from the handful of manufacturers and importers

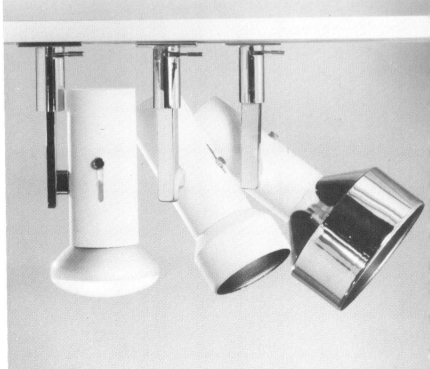

we've listed. Notice that many furniture manufacturers are now incorporating "task" and "ambient" light equipment in their product lines. These units often can be used separately, so they are worthy of consideration in some instances. Economy lamp products can cost as little as $20; some imports and floor standing "kiosks" may reach $350.

Accessories

Office furniture dealers and even some larger stationary stores carry letter trays, "organizers," ashtrays, desk pads, and similar items. Unfortunately, the design quality is variable. Useful gadgets of poor design can add to the needless sense of clutter in any office. Firms listed in this book specialize in providing better designs in good materials and colors. You can make selections from a catalog and ask the manufacturer to name a dealer who stocks or can order the item you need. Do not overlook retail design shops, department stores, and even kitchen shops as sources for well-designed accessories — often sold at low prices. A simple woven basket may be a better trash receptacle than an expensive leather wastebasket from an office furniture store. This is an area in which there is no consistency or logic in pricing, but value is fairly easy to determine on inspection.

Desk accessories sold by Peter Pepper Products (below). Planters for live plants available from Glassform (upper right). Wall clocks (upper far right) from Peter Pepper Products. Desk accessories (below right) from Eldon Office Products.

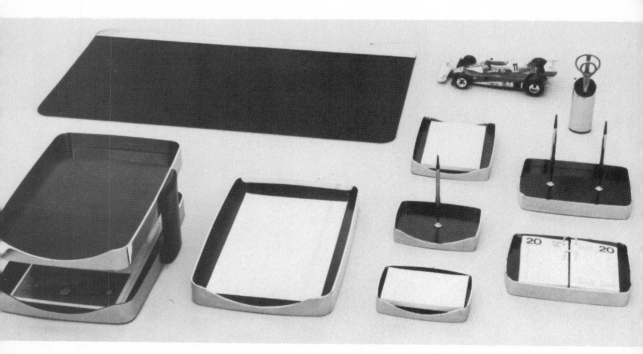

164

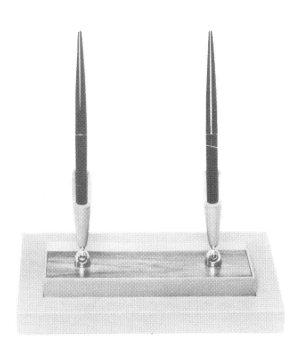

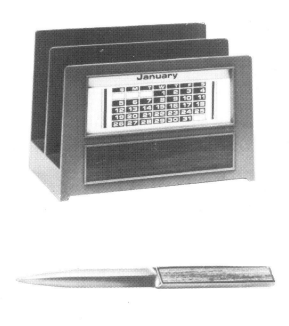

Art and Framing

This is an area so personal as to make standard recomendations almost impossible. Good galleries are concentrated in a few major cities, and each represents a "stable" of artists of some reputation. Large major works by known artists are often very expensive. Smaller works, drawings, prints or water colors are much less expensive and are often better suited in size and character to office use. Some galleries and dealers specialize in prints. Do not confuse reproductions which are printed in large quantities, with "original" prints which are printed by the artist or under his supervision in small quantities (25 to 200) and numbered. Prints are also often signed individually, or may bear a printed signature. Numbered and signed prints can appreciate just as one-of-a-kind paintings can. Signed and numbered prints by famous artists can be very costly, but are sometimes very good

Framed prints (below) often suit the character of an office. High-quality textiles such as Encounter I, a wall rug marketed by Edward Fields (right) is a pleasing alternative to the usual framed art work.

values. Do not overlook Oriental art (Japanese prints or Indian Tantric works, for example) or the use of textiles or other woven materials, maps, old prints, lithographs, and similar alternatives to the usual framed painting.

Important art works will usually be framed by the artist or gallery, or the gallery will be glad to arrange for framing. Any art store can do custom framing, but there are now many excellent ready-made frames and framing systems available as well. Thin and simple frames of white or black metal, or thin wood stripping, looks best on modern works, maps, prints, and photographs. Frames should never be more important than the work they contain. Ready-made frames make it easy to change the material displayed in your office as you add to your collection.

Modest prints, maps, and similar works can be found framed with prices starting at about $50 and ranging upward to several hundred dollars. Even small works by artists of some note can range upward from $200 or $300 into the thousands. And a major painting by an artist of even minor reputation is likely to cost $3000 to $5000 or more.

Evaluation And Planning

We have developed the charts on the following pages to show the relationships between specific office design elements and the abstract qualities that may be projected by those elements.

These charts list factors that usually enter into the design of any office in relation to the atmosphere they are likely to create. You can use these charts as a guide to selecting elements that will best convey your intentions. You can use them to evaluate and improve the office you have now.

You may include some elements that might seem contrary to your overall intentions if you have good reason to do so. But remember that the various details will interact and have a cumulative effect. One or two incongruous details may help you to establish your personality. But if too many elements are at odds with one another, the result could hamper rather than enhance your success.

Note that the descriptive term at the top of each chart is followed by two columns of factors that affect the environmental quality of offices. Next to each item on the lists is a symbol that designates the importance of each factor in the design of an office as it relates to the descriptive term.

The symbols are:

    ▲▲ Strongly significant
    ▲ Significant
    ○ Neutral
    ▽ Negative significance
    ▽▽ Strongly negative

So, for example, if you desire a formal office, look at the chart that has the word **Formal** at the top. Read down the list of factors and note the symbols. The first entry on the list is "size." You can see that large size is strongly significant, since this factor is given a ▲▲ symbol. Read down to the *Exposed beams and ducts* entry and see that this factor would be strongly negative (given a ▽▽ symbol) in an office for which a formal atmosphere is desired.

You can use the charts in several ways.

1. To see the relationships between the qualities you want to project (or avoid projecting) and the elements of office design that you might use (or avoid using). You can do this by simply scanning the lists. For example, you can see that a *Symmetrical* layout looks **Formal**, **Traditional**, and **Conservative** because it is given a ▲▲ symbol in those three charts.

2. To evaluate your office as it is now. Flip through the charts, looking at each listing and its symbol until you find a ▲▲ or a ▲ symbol next to a listing of a component of your office. For example, you might have *Exposed beams and ducts* in your office. The only chart that contains a ▲▲ symbol next to that component is **Economical.** Circle that symbol with a colored pencil. Then look up some of the other components of your office and see whether they too generate a feeling of economy more so than any other quality. If you find that your ▲▲ and ▲ scores are scattered among several different adjectives, you'll know that your office does not project any distinct qualities very strongly but instead is a more random mix of characteristics. This is not unusual.

3. To plan a new office. Use much the same procedure as is used for evaluation of an existing office. Find the chart headed by the description that best represents the quality you'd like your office to project. For example, you might want a **Formal** office. Read down the list of factors, marking with your colored pencil those that you can use to project a feeling of formality. You'll also be able to determine which components you should shun. To create a formal office, you'll want a large space, a symmetrical layout, paneled walls, incandescent recessed lighting, etc.— all factors marked with a ▲▲ symbol. Other factors that are only slightly less significant than these in projecting formality are marked with a ▲ symbol. You should avoid tile flooring if you want a formal-looking office, since tile is marked with a ▽ symbol.

Formal

SIZE:

Large (over 300 sq. ft.)	▲▲
Medium (100-300 sq. ft.)	▲
Small (100 sq. ft. or less)	○

LOCATION:

Corner	○
Window-wall	○
Inside	▽

SHAPE:

Square	▲
Near-square rectangle	▲
Long and narrow	○
Irregular	▽
Curved or round	▽

LAYOUT:

Symmetrical	▲▲
Non-symmetrical	○
Irregular	▽

WINDOWS:

None	○
One (small)	▲
Two or more	▲
Corner	▲
Glass wall	▲
Window to other offices	▽

VIEW:

Good to excellent	▲
Indifferent to poor	▽

WINDOW TREATMENT:

Venetian blinds	▲
Vertical louvers	○
Drapery	▲

WALLS:

Paint	▲
Vinyl wall covering	▲
Fabric or paper	▲
Paneling	▲▲
Mirror	▽

FLOORS:

Resilient tile or sheet	▽

FLOORS: (continued)

Carpet	▲
Rug or rugs	▲
Hardwood, parquet	▲

CEILING:

Exposed beams/ducts	▽▽
Acoustical tile	▽
Integrated system	▽
Plaster	○

LIGHTING:

Fluorescent, standard	▽
Fluorscent, low-bright	▲
Incandescent, recessed	▲▲
Indirect	▲
Lamps	▲

FURNITURE:

Desk:	
Large	▲
Small	○
Closed-front	▲▲
Open, or table	▽
Curved or round	▽▽
No desk (work counter)	▽
Conference table:	
rectangular	▲
round	▽
Lounge seating:	
2 or 3 chairs	○
sofa and table group	▲

COLORS:

Warm:	
Reds and pinks	○
Oranges	○
Yellows	○
Cool:	
Greens	○
Blues	○
Violets and purples	▽
Neutral:	
White	▲
Grays	▲▲

COLORS: (continued)

Black	▲
Browns	▲▲
Tans and beiges	▲▲

TEXTURES:

Smooth, slick, shiny	▽
Natural, fuzzy, heavy	○
Metallics	▽

STYLES:

Traditional:	
Gothic/Tudor	▲
Georgian/Colonial	▲▲
Victorian	▽
French periods	▽
Modern:	
Contemporary	▲
Bauhaus	▲
Art Deco	▽
High Tech	▽
Mixed styles	▽

ACCESSORIES:

Souvenirs/mementos	○
Family pictures	○
Maps and charts	▲
Models (ships, RR, etc.)	○
Business charts	▲
Tackboard/chalk board	○
Books and shelves	▲▲
Bar	○
TV or film projection	○
Posters	▽
Photos/advertisements	▽
Prints (original art)	○
Small water color	▲
Small oil painting	▲
Major oil painting(s)	▲
Many small art works	▲
Diplomas or certificates	▲
Plants	▲
Cut flowers	▲

▲▲ *Strongly significant*   ▲ *Significant*   ○ *Neutral*   ▽ *Negative significance*   ▽▽ *Strongly negative*

Informal

SIZE:	
Large (over 300 sq. ft.)	▽
Medium (100-300 sq. ft.)	○
Small (100 sq. ft. or less)	▲

LOCATION:	
Corner	○
Window-wall	○
Inside	○

SHAPE:	
Square	○
Near-square rectangle	○
Long and narrow	○
Irregular	▲
Curved or round	▲

LAYOUT:	
Symmetrical	▽
Non-symmetrical	▲
Irregular	▲▲

WINDOWS:	
None	○
One (small)	○
Two or more	○
Corner	○
Glass wall	○
Window to other offices	▲

VIEW:	
Good to excellent	○
Indifferent to poor	▲

WINDOW TREATMENT:	
Venetian blinds	○
Vertical louvers	▲
Drapery	▲

WALLS:	
Paint	▲
Vinyl wall covering	▲
Fabric or paper	▲
Paneling	▽
Mirror	○

FLOORS:	
Resilient tile or sheet	▲

FLOORS: (continued)	
Carpet	▲
Rug or rugs	▲
Hardwood, parquet	○

CEILING:	
Exposed beams/ducts	▲
Acoustical tile	▲
Integrated system	▲
Plaster	○

LIGHTING:	
Fluorescent, standard	▲
Fluorscent, low-bright	○
Incandescent, recessed	○
Indirect	○
Lamps	▲

FURNITURE:	
Desk:	
Large	▽
Small	▲
Closed-front	○
Open, or table	▲▲
Curved or round	▲
No desk (work counter)	▲
Conference table:	
rectangular	▲
round	▲▲
Lounge seating:	
2 or 3 chairs	▲
sofa and table group	▲

COLORS:	
Warm:	
Reds and pinks	▲
Oranges	▲
Yellows	▲
Cool:	
Greens	○
Blues	○
Violets and purples	○
Neutral:	
White	▲
Grays	○

COLORS: (continued)	
Black	○
Browns	▲
Tans and beiges	▲

TEXTURES:	
Smooth, slick, shiny	○
Natural, fuzzy, heavy	▲▲
Metallics	▲

STYLES:	
Traditional:	
Gothic/Tudor	▽
Georgian/Colonial	▽
Victorian	▲
French periods	○
Modern:	
Contemporary	▲▲
Bauhaus	▲
Art Deco	▲
High Tech	▲
Mixed styles	▲▲

ACCESSORIES:	
Souvenirs/mementos	▲▲
Family pictures	▲
Maps and charts	▲
Models (ships, RR, etc.)	▲
Business charts	▲
Tackboard/chalk board	▲
Books and shelves	▲
Bar	▲
TV or film projection	▲
Posters	▲
Photos/advertisements	▲
Prints (original art)	▲
Small water color	▲
Small oil painting	▲
Major oil painting(s)	○
Many small art works	▲
Diplomas or certificates	▲
Plants	▲▲
Cut flowers	▲▲

▲▲ *Strongly significant*   ▲ *Significant*   ○ *Neutral*   ▽ *Negative significance*   ▽▽ *Strongly negative*

Dignified

SIZE:	
Large (over 300 sq. ft.)	▲
Medium (100-300 sq. ft.)	O
Small (100 sq. ft. or less)	▽

LOCATION:	
Corner	▲
Window-wall	▲
Inside	O

SHAPE:	
Square	▲
Near-square rectangle	▲▲
Long and narrow	O
Irregular	▽
Curved or round	▽▽

LAYOUT:	
Symmetrical	▲
Non-symmetrical	O
Irregular	▽

WINDOWS:	
None	O
One (small)	▲
Two or more	▲
Corner	▲▲
Glass wall	▲
Window to other offices	O

VIEW:	
Good to excellent	▲
Indifferent to poor	O

WINDOW TREATMENT:	
Venetian blinds	▲
Vertical louvers	▲
Drapery	O

WALLS:	
Paint	O
Vinyl wall covering	O
Fabric or paper	▲
Paneling	▲▲
Mirror	O

FLOORS:	
Resilient tile or sheet	▽

FLOORS: (continued)	
Carpet	O
Rug or rugs	▲
Hardwood, parquet	▲

CEILING:	
Exposed beams/ducts	▽
Acoustical tile	O
Integrated system	O
Plaster	O

LIGHTING:	
Fluorescent, standard	O
Fluorscent, low-bright	▲
Incandescent, recessed	▲
Indirect	▲▲
Lamps	▲▲

FURNITURE:	
Desk:	
Large	▲▲
Small	▽
Closed-front	▲
Open, or table	O
Curved or round	▽
No desk (work counter)	O
Conference table:	
rectangular	▲
round	▽
Lounge seating:	
2 or 3 chairs	O
sofa and table group	▲

COLORS:	
Warm:	
Reds and pinks	▽
Oranges	▽▽
Yellows	▽
Cool:	
Greens	▽
Blues	▲
Violets and purples	O
Neutral:	
White	▲
Grays	▲

COLORS: (continued)	
Black	▲
Browns	▲▲
Tans and beiges	▲▲

TEXTURES:	
Smooth, slick, shiny	▽
Natural, fuzzy, heavy	O
Metallics	▽

STYLES:	
Traditional:	
Gothic/Tudor	▲
Georgian/Colonial	▲▲
Victorian	▽
French periods	▽
Modern:	
Contemporary	▲
Bauhaus	▲
Art Deco	O
High Tech	▽
Mixed styles	▽

ACCESSORIES:	
Souvenirs/mementos	O
Family pictures	O
Maps and charts	O
Models (ships, RR, etc.)	O
Business charts	O
Tackboard/chalk board	▽
Books and shelves	▲
Bar	O
TV or film projection	O
Posters	▽▽
Photos/advertisements	▽▽
Prints (original art)	▽
Small water color	O
Small oil painting	▲
Major oil painting(s)	▲
Many small art works	O
Diplomas or certificates	▲
Plants	▲
Cut flowers	▲

▲▲ *Strongly significant* ▲ *Significant* O *Neutral* ▽ *Negative significance* ▽▽ *Strongly negative*

Businesslike

SIZE:

Large (over 300 sq. ft.)	O
Medium (100-300 sq. ft.)	▲
Small (100 sq. ft. or less)	O

LOCATION:

Corner	O
Window-wall	O
Inside	O

SHAPE:

Square	▲
Near-square rectangle	▲
Long and narrow	O
Irregular	▽
Curved or round	▽▽

LAYOUT:

Symmetrical	▲
Non-symmetrical	O
Irregular	▽

WINDOWS:

None	O
One (small)	▲
Two or more	▲
Corner	▲▲
Glass wall	▲
Window to other offices	▲

VIEW:

Good to excellent	O
Indifferent to poor	▽

WINDOW TREATMENT:

Venetian blinds	▲▲
Vertical louvers	▲
Drapery	O

WALLS:

Paint	▲
Vinyl wall covering	▲
Fabric or paper	O
Paneling	▲
Mirror	▽

FLOORS:

Resilient tile or sheet	▲

FLOORS: (continued)

Carpet	▲
Rug or rugs	O
Hardwood, parquet	O

CEILING:

Exposed beams/ducts	▽
Acoustical tile	▲
Integrated system	▲
Plaster	O

LIGHTING:

Fluorescent, standard	▲
Fluorscent, low-bright	O
Incandescent, recessed	O
Indirect	▽
Lamps	▽

FURNITURE:

Desk:	
Large	▲
Small	O
Closed-front	▲
Open, or table	O
Curved or round	▽
No desk (work counter)	O
Conference table:	
rectangular	▲
round	▲
Lounge seating:	
2 or 3 chairs	▲
sofa and table group	▲

COLORS:

Warm:	
Reds and pinks	O
Oranges	O
Yellows	▲
Cool:	
Greens	▲
Blues	O
Violets and purples	▽
Neutral:	
White	▲
Grays	▲

COLORS: (continued)

Black	▲
Browns	▲
Tans and beiges	▲

TEXTURES:

Smooth, slick, shiny	O
Natural, fuzzy, heavy	▽
Metallics	▽

STYLES:

Traditional:	
Gothic/Tudor	▽
Georgian/Colonial	▲
Victorian	▽
French periods	▽
Modern:	
Contemporary	▲
Bauhaus	▲
Art Deco	▽
High Tech	▽
Mixed styles	▽

ACCESSORIES:

Souvenirs/mementos	▲
Family pictures	▲
Maps and charts	▲
Models (ships, RR, etc.)	▲
Business charts	▲▲
Tackboard/chalk board	▲▲
Books and shelves	▲
Bar	O
TV or film projection	O
Posters	O
Photos/advertisements	▲
Prints (original art)	O
Small water color	O
Small oil painting	O
Major oil painting(s)	▽
Many small art works	O
Diplomas or certificates	▲
Plants	▲
Cut flowers	O

▲▲ *Strongly significant*   ▲*Significant*   O*Neutral*   ▽*Negative significance*   ▽▽*Strongly negative*

Professional

SIZE:

Large (over 300 sq. ft.)	▽
Medium (100-300 sq. ft.)	▲
Small (100 sq. ft. or less)	○

LOCATION:

Corner	▲
Window-wall	▲
Inside	○

SHAPE:

Square	▲
Near-square rectangle	▲
Long and narrow	○
Irregular	▽
Curved or round	▽▽

LAYOUT:

Symmetrical	▲
Non-symmetrical	○
Irregular	▽

WINDOWS:

None	○
One (small)	▲
Two or more	▲
Corner	▲
Glass wall	○
Window to other offices	▽

VIEW:

Good to excellent	○
Indifferent to poor	▽

WINDOW TREATMENT:

Venetian blinds	▲
Vertical louvers	○
Drapery	▽

WALLS:

Paint	▲
Vinyl wall covering	▲▲
Fabric or paper	▽
Paneling	▽
Mirror	▽▽

FLOORS:

Resilient tile or sheet	▲

FLOORS: (continued)

Carpet	▲
Rug or rugs	○
Hardwood, parquet	○

CEILING:

Exposed beams/ducts	▽
Acoustical tile	▲
Integrated system	▲
Plaster	▲

LIGHTING:

Fluorescent, standard	▲
Fluorscent, low-bright	▲
Incandescent, recessed	▲
Indirect	○
Lamps	○

FURNITURE:

Desk:	
Large	▲
Small	○
Closed-front	▲
Open, or table	○
Curved or round	▽
No desk (work counter)	○
Conference table:	
rectangular	▲
round	▲
Lounge seating:	
2 or 3 chairs	▲
sofa and table group	○

COLORS:

Warm:	
Reds and pinks	▽
Oranges	▽
Yellows	○
Cool:	
Greens	○
Blues	○
Violets and purples	▽
Neutral:	
White	▲
Grays	▲

COLORS: (continued)

Black	○
Browns	○
Tans and beiges	▲

TEXTURES:

Smooth, slick, shiny	○
Natural, fuzzy, heavy	○
Metallics	○

STYLES:

Traditional:	
Gothic/Tudor	▽
Georgian/Colonial	▲
Victorian	▽
French periods	▽
Modern:	
Contemporary	▲▲
Bauhaus	▲
Art Deco	▲
High Tech	▲▲
Mixed styles	▽

ACCESSORIES:

Souvenirs/mementos	▲
Family pictures	▲
Maps and charts	▲
Models (ships, RR, etc.)	▲
Business charts	▲
Tackboard/chalk board	○
Books and shelves	▲▲
Bar	▽
TV or film projection	▽
Posters	▽
Photos/advertisements	▽
Prints (original art)	○
Small water color	▲
Small oil painting	▲
Major oil painting(s)	○
Many small art works	○
Diplomas or certificates	▲▲
Plants	▲
Cut flowers	▲

▲▲ *Strongly significant*   ▲ *Significant*   ○ *Neutral*   ▽ *Negative significance*   ▽▽ *Strongly negative*

Intellectual

SIZE:

Large (over 300 sq. ft.)	○
Medium (100-300 sq. ft.)	○
Small (100 sq. ft. or less)	○

LOCATION:

Corner	○
Window-wall	○
Inside	○

SHAPE:

Square	○
Near-square rectangle	○
Long and narrow	○
Irregular	▲
Curved or round	▲

LAYOUT:

Symmetrical	○
Non-symmetrical	▲
Irregular	▲

WINDOWS:

None	▲
One (small)	▲
Two or more	▲
Corner	○
Glass wall	○
Window to other offices	○

VIEW:

Good to excellent	○
Indifferent to poor	▽

WINDOW TREATMENT:

Venetian blinds	○
Vertical louvers	▲
Drapery	○

WALLS:

Paint	▲
Vinyl wall covering	▲
Fabric or paper	○
Paneling	▽
Mirror	▽▽

FLOORS:

Resilient tile or sheet	○

FLOORS: (continued)

Carpet	○
Rug or rugs	○
Hardwood, parquet	▲

CEILING:

Exposed beams/ducts	○
Acoustical tile	○
Integrated system	○
Plaster	○

LIGHTING:

Fluorescent, standard	○
Fluorscent, low-bright	▲
Incandescent, recessed	▲
Indirect	○
Lamps	▲

FURNITURE:

Desk:	
Large	○
Small	▲
Closed-front	○
Open, or table	▲
Curved or round	○
No desk (work counter)	▲
Conference table:	
rectangular	○
round	▲
Lounge seating:	
2 or 3 chairs	○
sofa and table group	○

COLORS:

Warm:	
Reds and pinks	○
Oranges	○
Yellows	▲
Cool:	
Greens	○
Blues	▲
Violets and purples	▲
Neutral:	
White	▲▲
Grays	▲

COLORS: (continued)

Black	▲
Browns	▲
Tans and beiges	▲

TEXTURES:

Smooth, slick, shiny	○
Natural, fuzzy, heavy	▲
Metallics	▽

STYLES:

Traditional:	
Gothic/Tudor	▽
Georgian/Colonial	▽
Victorian	▽
French periods	▽
Modern:	
Contemporary	▲
Bauhaus	▲▲
Art Deco	▲
High Tech	▲
Mixed styles	○

ACCESSORIES:

Souvenirs/mementos	○
Family pictures	○
Maps and charts	▲
Models (ships, RR, etc.)	○
Business charts	▲
Tackboard/chalk board	▲
Books and shelves	▲▲
Bar	▽▽
TV or film projection	▽
Posters	▽
Photos/advertisements	▽
Prints (original art)	○
Small water color	○
Small oil painting	○
Major oil painting(s)	▽
Many small art works	▲
Diplomas or certificates	▲▲
Plants	▲
Cut flowers	○

▲▲*Strongly significant*   ▲*Significant*   ○*Neutral*   ▽*Negative significance*   ▽▽*Strongly negative*

Creative

SIZE:
Large (over 300 sq. ft.)	O
Medium (100-300 sq. ft.)	▲
Small (100 sq. ft. or less)	▲

LOCATION:
Corner	▲
Window-wall	▲
Inside	O

SHAPE:
Square	O
Near-square rectangle	O
Long and narrow	O
Irregular	▲
Curved or round	▲▲

LAYOUT:
Symmetrical	O
Non-symmetrical	▲
Irregular	▲▲

WINDOWS:
None	O
One (small)	O
Two or more	O
Corner	O
Glass wall	▲
Window to other offices	▲

VIEW:
Good to excellent	▲
Indifferent to poor	▽

WINDOW TREATMENT:
Venetian blinds	O
Vertical louvers	▲
Drapery	▲

WALLS:
Paint	▲
Vinyl wall covering	▲
Fabric or paper	O
Paneling	▽
Mirror	▽▽

FLOORS:
Resilient tile or sheet	O

FLOORS: (continued)
Carpet	O
Rug or rugs	▲
Hardwood, parquet	▲

CEILING:
Exposed beams/ducts	▲
Acoustical tile	O
Integrated system	O
Plaster	O

LIGHTING:
Fluorescent, standard	▽
Fluorscent, low-bright	▲
Incandescent, recessed	▲
Indirect	O
Lamps	▲

FURNITURE:
Desk:	
Large	O
Small	O
Closed-front	O
Open, or table	▲
Curved or round	▲
No desk (work counter)	▲
Conference table:	
rectangular	O
round	▲
Lounge seating:	
2 or 3 chairs	O
sofa and table group	O

COLORS:
Warm:	
Reds and pinks	▲
Oranges	▲
Yellows	O
Cool:	
Greens	▽
Blues	O
Violets and purples	▲
Neutral:	
White	▲▲
Grays	▲

COLORS: (continued)
Black	▲
Browns	▲
Tans and beiges	▲

TEXTURES:
Smooth, slick, shiny	▲
Natural, fuzzy, heavy	▲
Metallics	▲

STYLES:
Traditional:	
Gothic/Tudor	▽▽
Georgian/Colonial	▽▽
Victorian	▽▽
French periods	▽▽
Modern:	
Contemporary	▲
Bauhaus	▲▲
Art Deco	▲
High Tech	▲▲
Mixed styles	▲

ACCESSORIES:
Souvenirs/mementos	▲
Family pictures	▲
Maps and charts	▲
Models (ships, RR, etc.)	▲
Business charts	O
Tackboard/chalk board	▲▲
Books and shelves	▲▲
Bar	▽
TV or film projection	▲
Posters	O
Photos/advertisements	▲
Prints (original art)	▲
Small water color	▲
Small oil painting	▲
Major oil painting(s)	O
Many small art works	O
Diplomas or certificates	▲
Plants	▲
Cut flowers	O

▲▲ *Strongly significant*   ▲ *Significant*   O *Neutral*   ▽ *Negative significance*   ▽▽ *Strongly negative*

SIZE:

Large (over 300 sq. ft.)	O
Medium (100-300 sq. ft.)	▲
Small (100 sq. ft. or less)	▲

LOCATION:

Corner	O
Window-wall	O
Inside	O

SHAPE:

Square	O
Near-square rectangle	O
Long and narrow	O
Irregular	▲
Curved or round	▲▲

LAYOUT:

Symmetrical	O
Non-symmetrical	▲
Irregular	▲▲

WINDOWS:

None	O
One (small)	O
Two or more	O
Corner	O
Glass wall	▲
Window to other offices	▲

VIEW:

Good to excellent	O
Indifferent to poor	▽

WINDOW TREATMENT:

Venetian blinds	O
Vertical louvers	▲
Drapery	O

WALLS:

Paint	▲
Vinyl wall covering	▲
Fabric or paper	▽
Paneling	▽
Mirror	▽▽

FLOORS:

Resilient tile or sheet	O

FLOORS: (continued)

Carpet	▲
Rug or rugs	O
Hardwood, parquet	O

CEILING:

Exposed beams/ducts	▲
Acoustical tile	O
Integrated system	▲
Plaster	O

LIGHTING:

Fluorescent, standard	▽
Fluorscent, low-bright	▲
Incandescent, recessed	▲
Indirect	▲
Lamps	▲▲

FURNITURE:

Desk:	
Large	O
Small	O
Closed-front	▽
Open, or table	▲
Curved or round	▲▲
No desk (work counter)	▲▲
Conference table:	
rectangular	O
round	▲
Lounge seating:	
2 or 3 chairs	O
sofa and table group	O

COLORS:

Warm:	
Reds and pinks	▲
Oranges	▲
Yellows	▲
Cool:	
Greens	O
Blues	▲
Violets and purples	▲
Neutral:	
White	▲▲
Grays	▲

COLORS: (continued)

Black	O
Browns	O
Tans and beiges	▲

TEXTURES:

Smooth, slick, shiny	▲▲
Natural, fuzzy, heavy	▲
Metallics	▲

STYLES:

Traditional:	
Gothic/Tudor	▽▽
Georgian/Colonial	▽▽
Victorian	▽▽
French periods	▽▽
Modern:	
Contemporary	▲
Bauhaus	▲
Art Deco	▲
High Tech	▲▲
Mixed styles	▲

ACCESSORIES:

Souvenirs/mementos	▲
Family pictures	▲
Maps and charts	▲
Models (ships, RR, etc.)	▲
Business charts	▲
Tackboard/chalk board	▲▲
Books and shelves	▲▲
Bar	O
TV or film projection	▲
Posters	▲
Photos/advertisements	▲
Prints (original art)	▲
Small water color	▲
Small oil painting	O
Major oil painting(s)	O
Many small art works	O
Diplomas or certificates	▲
Plants	▲
Cut flowers	O

▲▲ *Strongly significant*　▲*Significant*　O*Neutral*　▽*Negative significance*　▽▽*Strongly negative*

Artistic

Column 1

SIZE:

Large (over 300 sq. ft.)	○
Medium (100-300 sq. ft.)	○
Small (100 sq. ft. or less)	○

LOCATION:

Corner	▲
Window-wall	▲
Inside	○

SHAPE:

Square	▲
Near-square rectangle	▲
Long and narrow	○
Irregular	▲
Curved or round	▲▲

LAYOUT:

Symmetrical	○
Non-symmetrical	▲
Irregular	▲▲

WINDOWS:

None	▽
One (small)	○
Two or more	▲
Corner	▲
Glass wall	▲▲
Window to other offices	○

VIEW:

Good to excellent	▲
Indifferent to poor	▽

WINDOW TREATMENT:

Venetian blinds	○
Vertical louvers	▲
Drapery	▲

WALLS:

Paint	▲
Vinyl wall covering	○
Fabric or paper	○
Paneling	▽
Mirror	▽▽

FLOORS:

Resilient tile or sheet	○

Column 2

FLOORS: (continued)

Carpet	○
Rug or rugs	▲
Hardwood, parquet	▲

CEILING:

Exposed beams/ducts	▲
Acoustical tile	○
Integrated system	○
Plaster	▲

LIGHTING:

Fluorescent, standard	▽▽
Fluorscent, low-bright	▲
Incandescent, recessed	▲
Indirect	▲
Lamps	▲▲

FURNITURE:

Desk:	
Large	○
Small	○
Closed-front	▽
Open, or table	▲
Curved or round	▲
No desk (work counter)	▲▲
Conference table:	
rectangular	○
round	▲
Lounge seating:	
2 or 3 chairs	○
sofa and table group	○

COLORS:

Warm:	
Reds and pinks	▲
Oranges	▲
Yellows	▲
Cool:	
Greens	○
Blues	▲
Violets and purples	▲
Neutral:	
White	▲▲
Grays	○

Column 3

COLORS: (continued)

Black	○
Browns	○
Tans and beiges	▲

TEXTURES:

Smooth, slick, shiny	▲
Natural, fuzzy, heavy	▲▲
Metallics	▲

STYLES:

Traditional:	
Gothic/Tudor	▽
Georgian/Colonial	▽
Victorian	▽
French periods	▽
Modern:	
Contemporary	▲
Bauhaus	▲
Art Deco	▲
High Tech	▲▲
Mixed styles	▲

ACCESSORIES:

Souvenirs/mementos	▲
Family pictures	▲
Maps and charts	▲
Models (ships, RR, etc.)	▲
Business charts	▽
Tackboard/chalk board	○
Books and shelves	▲
Bar	○
TV or film projection	▲
Posters	▲
Photos/advertisements	▲
Prints (original art)	▲
Small water color	▲
Small oil painting	▲
Major oil painting(s)	○
Many small art works	▲
Diplomas or certificates	○
Plants	▲
Cut flowers	○

▲▲ *Strongly significant*   ▲ *Significant*   ○ *Neutral*   ▽ *Negative significance*   ▽▽ *Strongly negative*

STATUS: High

SIZE:

Large (over 300 sq. ft.)	▲▲
Medium (100-300 sq. ft.)	▲
Small (100 sq. ft. or less)	O

LOCATION:

Corner	▲▲
Window-wall	▲
Inside	▽

SHAPE:

Square	▲
Near-square rectangle	▲
Long and narrow	O
Irregular	O
Curved or round	▲

LAYOUT:

Symmetrical	▲
Non-symmetrical	▲
Irregular	O

WINDOWS:

None	▽▽
One (small)	▽
Two or more	O
Corner	▲
Glass wall	▲
Window to other offices	▽

VIEW:

Good to excellent	▲
Indifferent to poor	▽▽

WINDOW TREATMENT:

Venetian blinds	O
Vertical louvers	▲▲
Drapery	▲▲

WALLS:

Paint	O
Vinyl wall covering	▲
Fabric or paper	▲
Paneling	▲▲
Mirror	▲

FLOORS:

Resilient tile or sheet	▽

FLOORS: (continued)

Carpet	O
Rug or rugs	▲▲
Hardwood, parquet	▲▲

CEILING:

Exposed beams/ducts	▽▽
Acoustical tile	▽
Integrated system	O
Plaster	▲

LIGHTING:

Fluorescent, standard	▽▽
Fluorscent, low-bright	▲
Incandescent, recessed	▲▲
Indirect	▲
Lamps	▲▲

FURNITURE:

Desk:	
Large	▲▲
Small	▽
Closed-front	▲
Open, or table	▲
Curved or round	▲
No desk (work counter)	O
Conference table:	
rectangular	O
round	▲
Lounge seating:	
2 or 3 chairs	▲
sofa and table group	▲▲

COLORS:

Warm:	
Reds and pinks	O
Oranges	▽▽
Yellows	▽▽
Cool:	
Greens	▽
Blues	O
Violets and purples	▽
Neutral:	
White	O
Grays	▲

COLORS: (continued)

Black	▲
Browns	▲▲
Tans and beiges	▲▲

TEXTURES:

Smooth, slick, shiny	▽
Natural, fuzzy, heavy	▲
Metallics	▽

STYLES:

Traditional:	
Gothic/Tudor	▲
Georgian/Colonial	▲▲
Victorian	O
French periods	▲
Modern:	
Contemporary	▲
Bauhaus	▲
Art Deco	O
High Tech	▲
Mixed styles	▽

ACCESSORIES:

Souvenirs/mementos	O
Family pictures	▽
Maps and charts	▽
Models (ships, RR, etc.)	▽
Business charts	▽▽
Tackboard/chalk board	▽▽
Books and shelves	▲
Bar	▲
TV or film projection	▲
Posters	▽▽
Photos/advertisements	▽▽
Prints (original art)	O
Small water color	▲
Small oil painting	▲
Major oil painting(s)	▲▲
Many small art works	▲
Diplomas or certificates	O
Plants	▲▲
Cut flowers	▲

▲▲ *Strongly significant*   ▲ *Significant*   O *Neutral*   ▽ *Negative significance*   ▽▽ *Strongly negative*

SIZE:

Large (over 300 sq. ft.)	▲
Medium (100-300 sq. ft.)	▲
Small (100 sq. ft. or less)	▽

LOCATION:

Corner	▲
Window-wall	○
Inside	▽

SHAPE:

Square	▲
Near-square rectangle	▲
Long and narrow	○
Irregular	○
Curved or round	○

LAYOUT:

Symmetrical	▲
Non-symmetrical	○
Irregular	▽

WINDOWS:

None	▽
One (small)	▲
Two or more	▲
Corner	▲
Glass wall	○
Window to other offices	○

VIEW:

Good to excellent	▲
Indifferent to poor	▽

WINDOW TREATMENT:

Venetian blinds	▲
Vertical louvers	▲
Drapery	▲

WALLS:

Paint	▲
Vinyl wall covering	▲
Fabric or paper	▲
Paneling	○
Mirror	○

FLOORS:

Resilient tile or sheet	○

FLOORS: (continued)

Carpet	▲
Rug or rugs	▲▲
Hardwood, parquet	▲▲

CEILING:

Exposed beams/ducts	▽
Acoustical tile	○
Integrated system	○
Plaster	○

LIGHTING:

Fluorescent, standard	○
Fluorscent, low-bright	○
Incandescent, recessed	○
Indirect	▽
Lamps	▲

FURNITURE:

Desk:	
Large	▲
Small	▲
Closed-front	▲
Open, or table	○
Curved or round	○
No desk (work counter)	○
Conference table:	
rectangular	▲
round	▲
Lounge seating:	
2 or 3 chairs	▲▲
sofa and table group	▲

COLORS:

Warm:	
Reds and pinks	○
Oranges	▽
Yellows	○
Cool:	
Greens	○
Blues	▽
Violets and purples	▽
Neutral:	
White	○
Grays	○

COLORS: (continued)

Black	○
Browns	▲
Tans and beiges	▲

TEXTURES:

Smooth, slick, shiny	○
Natural, fuzzy, heavy	▲
Metallics	○

STYLES:

Traditional:	
Gothic/Tudor	▽
Georgian/Colonial	▲
Victorian	▲
French periods	▽
Modern:	
Contemporary	▲
Bauhaus	▲
Art Deco	○
High Tech	○
Mixed styles	▽

ACCESSORIES:

Souvenirs/mementos	▲
Family pictures	▲
Maps and charts	▲
Models (ships, RR, etc.)	▲
Business charts	▲
Tackboard/chalk board	▲
Books and shelves	▲
Bar	○
TV or film projection	○
Posters	○
Photos/advertisements	○
Prints (original art)	▲
Small water color	▲
Small oil painting	▲
Major oil painting(s)	▽
Many small art works	○
Diplomas or certificates	○
Plants	▲
Cut flowers	○

▲▲ *Strongly significant*   ▲ *Significant*   ○ *Neutral*   ▽ *Negative significance*   ▽▽ *Strongly negative*

STATUS: Low

SIZE:	
Large (over 300 sq. ft.)	▽
Medium (100-300 sq. ft.)	O
Small (100 sq. ft. or less)	▲

LOCATION:	
Corner	O
Window-wall	O
Inside	▲

SHAPE:	
Square	O
Near-square rectangle	O
Long and narrow	▲
Irregular	▲
Curved or round	O

LAYOUT:	
Symmetrical	▲
Non-symmetrical	▽
Irregular	▽▽

WINDOWS:	
None	O
One (small)	▲
Two or more	▲
Corner	O
Glass wall	O
Window to other offices	▲

VIEW:	
Good to excellent	O
Indifferent to poor	▽

WINDOW TREATMENT:	
Venetian blinds	▲
Vertical louvers	O
Drapery	O

WALLS:	
Paint	▲
Vinyl wall covering	▲
Fabric or paper	O
Paneling	O
Mirror	O

FLOORS:	
Resilient tile or sheet	▲

FLOORS: (continued)	
Carpet	O
Rug or rugs	▽
Hardwood, parquet	▽

CEILING:	
Exposed beams/ducts	▲
Acoustical tile	▲
Integrated system	O
Plaster	O

LIGHTING:	
Fluorescent, standard	▲
Fluorscent, low-bright	O
Incandescent, recessed	O
Indirect	▽
Lamps	▽

FURNITURE:	
Desk:	
Large	▽
Small	▲▲
Closed-front	▲
Open, or table	▽
Curved or round	▽
No desk (work counter)	▽
Conference table:	
rectangular	▲
round	O
Lounge seating:	
2 or 3 chairs	O
sofa and table group	▽

COLORS:	
Warm:	
Reds and pinks	O
Oranges	O
Yellows	▲
Cool:	
Greens	▲
Blues	▲
Violets and purples	▽
Neutral:	
White	▽
Grays	▽

COLORS: (continued)	
Black	▽
Browns	O
Tans and beiges	▲

TEXTURES:	
Smooth, slick, shiny	O
Natural, fuzzy, heavy	▲
Metallics	▽

STYLES:	
Traditional:	
Gothic/Tudor	▽
Georgian/Colonial	O
Victorian	O
French periods	▽
Modern:	
Contemporary	▲
Bauhaus	O
Art Deco	O
High Tech	O
Mixed styles	O

ACCESSORIES:	
Souvenirs/mementos	▲
Family pictures	▲
Maps and charts	▲
Models (ships, RR, etc.)	O
Business charts	▲
Tackboard/chalk board	▲
Books and shelves	O
Bar	▽
TV or film projection	▽
Posters	▲
Photos/advertisements	▲
Prints (original art)	O
Small water color	O
Small oil painting	O
Major oil painting(s)	▽▽
Many small art works	▽
Diplomas or certificates	O
Plants	O
Cut flowers	O

▲▲ *Strongly significant*   ▲ *Significant*   O *Neutral*   ▽ *Negative significance*   ▽▽ *Strongly negative*

Organized

SIZE:	
Large (over 300 sq. ft.)	O
Medium (100-300 sq. ft.)	O
Small (100 sq. ft. or less)	O

LOCATION:	
Corner	O
Window-wall	O
Inside	O

SHAPE:	
Square	▲
Near-square rectangle	▲
Long and narrow	O
Irregular	▽
Curved or round	▽

LAYOUT:	
Symmetrical	▲
Non-symmetrical	O
Irregular	▽

WINDOWS:	
None	O
One (small)	O
Two or more	O
Corner	O
Glass wall	O
Window to other offices	O

VIEW:	
Good to excellent	O
Indifferent to poor	O

WINDOW TREATMENT:	
Venetian blinds	▲
Vertical louvers	▲
Drapery	O

WALLS:	
Paint	▲
Vinyl wall covering	▲
Fabric or paper	O
Paneling	O
Mirror	▽

FLOORS:	
Resilient tile or sheet	▲

FLOORS: (continued)	
Carpet	▲
Rug or rugs	O
Hardwood, parquet	O

CEILING:	
Exposed beams/ducts	▽
Acoustical tile	▲
Integrated system	▲
Plaster	O

LIGHTING:	
Fluorescent, standard	▲
Fluorscent, low-bright	▲
Incandescent, recessed	O
Indirect	O
Lamps	O

FURNITURE:	
Desk:	
Large	O
Small	▲
Closed-front	▲
Open, or table	O
Curved or round	▽
No desk (work counter)	▲
Conference table:	
rectangular	▲
round	▲
Lounge seating:	
2 or 3 chairs	▲
sofa and table group	▲

COLORS:	
Warm:	
Reds and pinks	▽
Oranges	▽
Yellows	O
Cool:	
Greens	▲
Blues	▲
Violets and purples	▽
Neutral:	
White	▲
Grays	▲

COLORS: (continued)	
Black	▲
Browns	▲
Tans and beiges	▲

TEXTURES:	
Smooth, slick, shiny	▲
Natural, fuzzy, heavy	O
Metallics	O

STYLES:	
Traditional:	
Gothic/Tudor	▽
Georgian/Colonial	O
Victorian	▽
French periods	▽
Modern:	
Contemporary	▲
Bauhaus	▲
Art Deco	O
High Tech	▲
Mixed styles	O

ACCESSORIES:	
Souvenirs/mementos	▲
Family pictures	▲
Maps and charts	▲
Models (ships, RR, etc.)	O
Business charts	▲▲
Tackboard/chalk board	▲▲
Books and shelves	▲
Bar	▽
TV or film projection	▽
Posters	O
Photos/advertisements	▲
Prints (original art)	O
Small water color	O
Small oil painting	O
Major oil painting(s)	O
Many small art works	O
Diplomas or certificates	▲
Plants	O
Cut flowers	O

▲▲ *Strongly significant*   ▲ *Significant*   O *Neutral*   ▽ *Negative significance*   ▽▽ *Strongly negative*

Systematic

SIZE:	
Large (over 300 sq. ft.)	O
Medium (100-300 sq. ft.)	O
Small (100 sq. ft. or less)	O
LOCATION:	
Corner	O
Window-wall	O
Inside	O
SHAPE:	
Square	▲
Near-square rectangle	▲
Long and narrow	O
Irregular	▽
Curved or round	▽
LAYOUT:	
Symmetrical	▲
Non-symmetrical	O
Irregular	▽
WINDOWS:	
None	O
One (small)	O
Two or more	O
Corner	O
Glass wall	O
Window to other offices	O
VIEW:	
Good to excellent	O
Indifferent to poor	O
WINDOW TREATMENT:	
Venetian blinds	▲
Vertical louvers	▲
Drapery	O
WALLS:	
Paint	▲
Vinyl wall covering	▲
Fabric or paper	O
Paneling	O
Mirror	▽
FLOORS:	
Resilient tile or sheet	▲

FLOORS: (continued)	
Carpet	▲
Rug or rugs	O
Hardwood, parquet	O
CEILING:	
Exposed beams/ducts	▽
Acoustical tile	▲
Integrated system	▲
Plaster	▲
LIGHTING:	
Fluorescent, standard	▲
Fluorscent, low-bright	▲
Incandescent, recessed	O
Indirect	O
Lamps	O
FURNITURE:	
Desk:	
Large	O
Small	▲
Closed-front	▲
Open, or table	O
Curved or round	▽
No desk (work counter)	▲
Conference table:	
rectangular	▲
round	▲
Lounge seating:	
2 or 3 chairs	▲
sofa and table group	▲
COLORS:	
Warm:	
Reds and pinks	▽
Oranges	▽
Yellows	O
Cool:	
Greens	▲▲
Blues	▲
Violets and purples	▽
Neutral:	
White	▲
Grays	▲

COLORS: (continued)	
Black	▲
Browns	▲
Tans and beiges	▲▲
TEXTURES:	
Smooth, slick, shiny	▲
Natural, fuzzy, heavy	▲
Metallics	O
STYLES:	
Traditional:	
Gothic/Tudor	▽
Georgian/Colonial	▽
Victorian	▽
French periods	▽
Modern:	
Contemporary	▲
Bauhaus	▲
Art Deco	▽
High Tech	O
Mixed styles	O
ACCESSORIES:	
Souvenirs/mementos	O
Family pictures	O
Maps and charts	▲
Models (ships, RR, etc.)	O
Business charts	▲
Tackboard/chalk board	▲
Books and shelves	▲
Bar	▽
TV or film projection	▽
Posters	▽
Photos/advertisements	O
Prints (original art)	O
Small water color	O
Small oil painting	▽
Major oil painting(s)	▽
Many small art works	▽
Diplomas or certificates	O
Plants	O
Cut flowers	O

▲▲ *Strongly significant*　▲*Significant*　O*Neutral*　▽*Negative significance*　▽▽*Strongly negative*

Bureaucratic

SIZE:	
Large (over 300 sq. ft.)	▽
Medium (100-300 sq. ft.)	O
Small (100 sq. ft. or less)	▲

LOCATION:	
Corner	O
Window-wall	O
Inside	▲

SHAPE:	
Square	▲
Near-square rectangle	▲
Long and narrow	O
Irregular	▽
Curved or round	▽▽

LAYOUT:	
Symmetrical	▲
Non-symmetrical	O
Irregular	▽

WINDOWS:	
None	▲
One (small)	▲
Two or more	▲
Corner	▽
Glass wall	▽
Window to other offices	▲

VIEW:	
Good to excellent	O
Indifferent to poor	O

WINDOW TREATMENT:	
Venetian blinds	▲▲
Vertical louvers	O
Drapery	▽

WALLS:	
Paint	▲
Vinyl wall covering	▲
Fabric or paper	▽
Paneling	▽
Mirror	▽

FLOORS:	
Resilient tile or sheet	▲▲

FLOORS: (continued)	
Carpet	▲
Rug or rugs	▽
Hardwood, parquet	▽▽

CEILING:	
Exposed beams/ducts	▲
Acoustical tile	▲
Integrated system	▲
Plaster	O

LIGHTING:	
Fluorescent, standard	▲▲
Fluorscent, low-bright	▲
Incandescent, recessed	O
Indirect	O
Lamps	▽

FURNITURE:	
Desk:	
Large	O
Small	▲
Closed-front	▲
Open, or table	▽
Curved or round	▽▽
No desk (work counter)	O
Conference table:	
rectangular	▲
round	O
Lounge seating:	
2 or 3 chairs	▲
sofa and table group	O

COLORS:	
Warm:	
Reds and pinks	▽
Oranges	▽▽
Yellows	O
Cool:	
Greens	▲▲
Blues	▲
Violets and purples	▽
Neutral:	
White	▲
Grays	▲

COLORS: (continued)	
Black	▲
Browns	▲
Tans and beiges	▲▲

TEXTURES:	
Smooth, slick, shiny	O
Natural, fuzzy, heavy	▲
Metallics	O

STYLES:	
Traditional:	
Gothic/Tudor	▽
Georgian/Colonial	O
Victorian	▽
French periods	▽
Modern:	
Contemporary	▲
Bauhaus	O
Art Deco	▽
High Tech	O
Mixed styles	O

ACCESSORIES:	
Souvenirs/mementos	O
Family pictures	O
Maps and charts	▲
Models (ships, RR, etc.)	O
Business charts	▲
Tackboard/chalk board	▲
Books and shelves	O
Bar	▽
TV or film projection	▽
Posters	▽
Photos/advertisements	O
Prints (original art)	▽
Small water color	▽
Small oil painting	▽
Major oil painting(s)	▽
Many small art works	O
Diplomas or certificates	O
Plants	O
Cut flowers	▽

▲▲ *Strongly significant*   ▲*Significant*   O*Neutral*   ▽*Negative significance*   ▽▽*Strongly negative*

Institutional

SIZE:	
Large (over 300 sq. ft.)	▽
Medium (100-300 sq. ft.)	O
Small (100 sq. ft. or less)	▲

LOCATION:	
Corner	O
Window-wall	O
Inside	▲

SHAPE:	
Square	▲
Near-square rectangle	▲
Long and narrow	O
Irregular	▽
Curved or round	▽▽

LAYOUT:	
Symmetrical	▲
Non-symmetrical	O
Irregular	▽

WINDOWS:	
None	▲
One (small)	▲
Two or more	▲
Corner	▽
Glass wall	▽
Window to other offices	▲

VIEW:	
Good to excellent	O
Indifferent to poor	O

WINDOW TREATMENT:	
Venetian blinds	▲▲
Vertical louvers	▲
Drapery	O

WALLS:	
Paint	▲
Vinyl wall covering	▲▲
Fabric or paper	▽
Paneling	▽
Mirror	▽▽

FLOORS:	
Resilient tile or sheet	▲▲

FLOORS: (continued)	
Carpet	O
Rug or rugs	▽▽
Hardwood, parquet	▽▽

CEILING:	
Exposed beams/ducts	▲
Acoustical tile	▲▲
Integrated system	▲
Plaster	O

LIGHTING:	
Fluorescent, standard	▲
Fluorscent, low-bright	O
Incandescent, recessed	O
Indirect	O
Lamps	▲

FURNITURE:	
Desk:	
Large	O
Small	▲
Closed-front	▲
Open, or table	▽
Curved or round	▽▽
No desk (work counter)	O
Conference table:	
rectangular	▲
round	O
Lounge seating:	
2 or 3 chairs	▲
sofa and table group	O

COLORS:	
Warm:	
Reds and pinks	▽
Oranges	▽▽
Yellows	O
Cool:	
Greens	▲▲
Blues	▲
Violets and purples	▽
Neutral:	
White	▲
Grays	▲

COLORS: (continued)	
Black	O
Browns	▲
Tans and beiges	▲▲

TEXTURES:	
Smooth, slick, shiny	O
Natural, fuzzy, heavy	▲
Metallics	O

STYLES:	
Traditional:	
Gothic/Tudor	O
Georgian/Colonial	O
Victorian	O
French periods	▽
Modern:	
Contemporary	▲
Bauhaus	▲
Art Deco	O
High Tech	▲
Mixed styles	O

ACCESSORIES:	
Souvenirs/mementos	▲
Family pictures	▲
Maps and charts	O
Models (ships, RR, etc.)	▽
Business charts	O
Tackboard/chalk board	▲
Books and shelves	▲
Bar	▽
TV or film projection	O
Posters	O
Photos/advertisements	O
Prints (original art)	O
Small water color	O
Small oil painting	O
Major oil painting(s)	▽
Many small art works	O
Diplomas or certificates	▲
Plants	▲
Cut flowers	O

▲▲ *Strongly significant* ▲ *Significant* O *Neutral* ▽ *Negative significance* ▽▽ *Strongly negative*

Academic

SIZE:	
Large (over 300 sq. ft.)	▽
Medium (100-300 sq. ft.)	O
Small (100 sq. ft. or less)	▲

LOCATION:	
Corner	O
Window-wall	O
Inside	O

SHAPE:	
Square	▲
Near-square rectangle	▲
Long and narrow	O
Irregular	▽
Curved or round	▽

LAYOUT:	
Symmetrical	O
Non-symmetrical	▲
Irregular	▲

WINDOWS:	
None	▲
One (small)	▲
Two or more	O
Corner	▽
Glass wall	▽
Window to other offices	▲

VIEW:	
Good to excellent	▲
Indifferent to poor	▽

WINDOW TREATMENT:	
Venetian blinds	▲▲
Vertical louvers	▲
Drapery	O

WALLS:	
Paint	▲
Vinyl wall covering	▲
Fabric or paper	▽
Paneling	▽
Mirror	▽▽

FLOORS:	
Resilient tile or sheet	O

FLOORS: (continued)	
Carpet	O
Rug or rugs	▽
Hardwood, parquet	▽

CEILING:	
Exposed beams/ducts	▲
Acoustical tile	▲
Integrated system	O
Plaster	O

LIGHTING:	
Fluorescent, standard	▽▽
Fluorscent, low-bright	▲
Incandescent, recessed	▲
Indirect	▲
Lamps	▲▲

FURNITURE:	
Desk:	
Large	O
Small	▲
Closed-front	▲
Open, or table	O
Curved or round	O
No desk (work counter)	O
Conference table:	
rectangular	▲
round	O
Lounge seating:	
2 or 3 chairs	▲
sofa and table group	O

COLORS:	
Warm:	
Reds and pinks	▽
Oranges	▽
Yellows	O
Cool:	
Greens	O
Blues	O
Violets and purples	O
Neutral:	
White	▲
Grays	▲

COLORS: (continued)	
Black	O
Browns	▲
Tans and beiges	▲▲

TEXTURES:	
Smooth, slick, shiny	O
Natural, fuzzy, heavy	O
Metallics	O

STYLES:	
Traditional:	
Gothic/Tudor	▽
Georgian/Colonial	O
Victorian	O
French periods	▽
Modern:	
Contemporary	▲▲
Bauhaus	▲
Art Deco	O
High Tech	▲
Mixed styles	▲

ACCESSORIES:	
Souvenirs/mementos	▲
Family pictures	O
Maps and charts	▲
Models (ships, RR, etc.)	O
Business charts	O
Tackboard/chalk board	▲▲
Books and shelves	▲▲
Bar	▽
TV or film projection	▲
Posters	▲
Photos/advertisements	▲
Prints (original art)	▲
Small water color	▲
Small oil painting	▲
Major oil painting(s)	▽
Many small art works	O
Diplomas or certificates	▲▲
Plants	▲
Cut flowers	O

▲▲ *Strongly significant*   ▲ *Significant*   O *Neutral*   ▽ *Negative significance*   ▽▽ *Strongly negative*

Confidential

SIZE:	
Large (over 300 sq. ft.)	O
Medium (100-300 sq. ft.)	▲
Small (100 sq. ft. or less)	▲

LOCATION:	
Corner	O
Window-wall	▲
Inside	▲

SHAPE:	
Square	O
Near-square rectangle	O
Long and narrow	O
Irregular	O
Curved or round	O

LAYOUT:	
Symmetrical	O
Non-symmetrical	O
Irregular	▽

WINDOWS:	
None	▲
One (small)	▲
Two or more	▲
Corner	▲
Glass wall	▽
Window to other offices	▽▽

VIEW:	
Good to excellent	O
Indifferent to poor	O

WINDOW TREATMENT:	
Venetian blinds	O
Vertical louvers	▲
Drapery	▲

WALLS:	
Paint	▲
Vinyl wall covering	▲
Fabric or paper	▲
Paneling	▲
Mirror	▽

FLOORS:	
Resilient tile or sheet	▽

FLOORS: (continued)	
Carpet	▲
Rug or rugs	▲▲
Hardwood, parquet	▲

CEILING:	
Exposed beams/ducts	▽
Acoustical tile	▲
Integrated system	O
Plaster	▲

LIGHTING:	
Fluorescent, standard	▽▽
Fluorscent, low-bright	▽
Incandescent, recessed	▲
Indirect	O
Lamps	▲▲

FURNITURE:	
Desk:	
Large	O
Small	O
Closed-front	▽
Open, or table	O
Curved or round	▲
No desk (work counter)	O
Conference table:	
rectangular	O
round	O
Lounge seating:	
2 or 3 chairs	▲
sofa and table group	▲

COLORS:	
Warm:	
Reds and pinks	O
Oranges	▽
Yellows	O
Cool:	
Greens	▲
Blues	▲
Violets and purples	O
Neutral:	
White	▲
Grays	▲

COLORS: (continued)	
Black	▲
Browns	▲▲
Tans and beiges	▲▲

TEXTURES:	
Smooth, slick, shiny	▽
Natural, fuzzy, heavy	▲▲
Metallics	▽

STYLES:	
Traditional:	
Gothic/Tudor	▲
Georgian/Colonial	▲▲
Victorian	▲
French periods	▲
Modern:	
Contemporary	O
Bauhaus	O
Art Deco	▽
High Tech	▽▽
Mixed styles	▲

ACCESSORIES:	
Souvenirs/mementos	▲
Family pictures	▲
Maps and charts	O
Models (ships, RR, etc.)	O
Business charts	▽
Tackboard/chalk board	▽
Books and shelves	▲▲
Bar	▽
TV or film projection	▽▽
Posters	▽▽
Photos/advertisements	▽▽
Prints (original art)	O
Small water color	▲
Small oil painting	▲
Major oil painting(s)	O
Many small art works	▲
Diplomas or certificates	▲
Plants	▲
Cut flowers	▲

▲▲ *Strongly significant* ▲ *Significant* O *Neutral* ▽ *Negative significance* ▽▽ *Strongly negative*

Friendly

<table>
<tr><td colspan="2">SIZE:</td></tr>
<tr><td>Large (over 300 sq. ft.)</td><td>▲</td></tr>
<tr><td>Medium (100-300 sq. ft.)</td><td>▲</td></tr>
<tr><td>Small (100 sq. ft. or less)</td><td>O</td></tr>
<tr><td colspan="2">LOCATION:</td></tr>
<tr><td>Corner</td><td>▲</td></tr>
<tr><td>Window-wall</td><td>▲</td></tr>
<tr><td>Inside</td><td>O</td></tr>
<tr><td colspan="2">SHAPE:</td></tr>
<tr><td>Square</td><td>O</td></tr>
<tr><td>Near-square rectangle</td><td>O</td></tr>
<tr><td>Long and narrow</td><td>O</td></tr>
<tr><td>Irregular</td><td>▲</td></tr>
<tr><td>Curved or round</td><td>▲</td></tr>
<tr><td colspan="2">LAYOUT:</td></tr>
<tr><td>Symmetrical</td><td>O</td></tr>
<tr><td>Non-symmetrical</td><td>▲</td></tr>
<tr><td>Irregular</td><td>▲</td></tr>
<tr><td colspan="2">WINDOWS:</td></tr>
<tr><td>None</td><td>O</td></tr>
<tr><td>One (small)</td><td>▲</td></tr>
<tr><td>Two or more</td><td>▲</td></tr>
<tr><td>Corner</td><td>O</td></tr>
<tr><td>Glass wall</td><td>O</td></tr>
<tr><td>Window to other offices</td><td>▽</td></tr>
<tr><td colspan="2">VIEW:</td></tr>
<tr><td>Good to excellent</td><td>▲</td></tr>
<tr><td>Indifferent to poor</td><td>O</td></tr>
<tr><td colspan="2">WINDOW TREATMENT:</td></tr>
<tr><td>Venetian blinds</td><td>▲</td></tr>
<tr><td>Vertical louvers</td><td>▲</td></tr>
<tr><td>Drapery</td><td>▲▲</td></tr>
<tr><td colspan="2">WALLS:</td></tr>
<tr><td>Paint</td><td>O</td></tr>
<tr><td>Vinyl wall covering</td><td>O</td></tr>
<tr><td>Fabric or paper</td><td>▲</td></tr>
<tr><td>Paneling</td><td>▲</td></tr>
<tr><td>Mirror</td><td>O</td></tr>
<tr><td colspan="2">FLOORS:</td></tr>
<tr><td>Resilient tile or sheet</td><td>▽</td></tr>
</table>

<table>
<tr><td colspan="2">FLOORS: (continued)</td></tr>
<tr><td>Carpet</td><td>▲</td></tr>
<tr><td>Rug or rugs</td><td>▲▲</td></tr>
<tr><td>Hardwood, parquet</td><td>▲</td></tr>
<tr><td colspan="2">CEILING:</td></tr>
<tr><td>Exposed beams/ducts</td><td>▽</td></tr>
<tr><td>Acoustical tile</td><td>▽</td></tr>
<tr><td>Integrated system</td><td>▽</td></tr>
<tr><td>Plaster</td><td>▲</td></tr>
<tr><td colspan="2">LIGHTING:</td></tr>
<tr><td>Fluorescent, standard</td><td>▽▽</td></tr>
<tr><td>Fluorscent, low-bright</td><td>▽</td></tr>
<tr><td>Incandescent, recessed</td><td>▲</td></tr>
<tr><td>Indirect</td><td>▲</td></tr>
<tr><td>Lamps</td><td>▲▲</td></tr>
<tr><td colspan="2">FURNITURE:</td></tr>
<tr><td>Desk:</td><td></td></tr>
<tr><td>   Large</td><td>▽</td></tr>
<tr><td>   Small</td><td>▲</td></tr>
<tr><td>   Closed-front</td><td>▽</td></tr>
<tr><td>   Open, or table</td><td>▲</td></tr>
<tr><td>   Curved or round</td><td>▲</td></tr>
<tr><td>No desk (work counter)</td><td>▲</td></tr>
<tr><td>Conference table:</td><td></td></tr>
<tr><td>   rectangular</td><td>O</td></tr>
<tr><td>   round</td><td>▲</td></tr>
<tr><td>Lounge seating:</td><td></td></tr>
<tr><td>   2 or 3 chairs</td><td>▲</td></tr>
<tr><td>   sofa and table group</td><td>▲▲</td></tr>
<tr><td colspan="2">COLORS:</td></tr>
<tr><td>Warm:</td><td></td></tr>
<tr><td>   Reds and pinks</td><td>▲</td></tr>
<tr><td>   Oranges</td><td>▲</td></tr>
<tr><td>   Yellows</td><td>▲</td></tr>
<tr><td>Cool:</td><td></td></tr>
<tr><td>   Greens</td><td>▲</td></tr>
<tr><td>   Blues</td><td>▲</td></tr>
<tr><td>   Violets and purples</td><td>O</td></tr>
<tr><td>Neutral:</td><td></td></tr>
<tr><td>   White</td><td>▲</td></tr>
<tr><td>   Grays</td><td>O</td></tr>
</table>

<table>
<tr><td colspan="2">COLORS: (continued)</td></tr>
<tr><td>Black</td><td>▽</td></tr>
<tr><td>Browns</td><td>▲</td></tr>
<tr><td>Tans and beiges</td><td>▲</td></tr>
<tr><td colspan="2">TEXTURES:</td></tr>
<tr><td>Smooth, slick, shiny</td><td>▽</td></tr>
<tr><td>Natural, fuzzy, heavy</td><td>▲</td></tr>
<tr><td>Metallics</td><td>▽</td></tr>
<tr><td colspan="2">STYLES:</td></tr>
<tr><td>Traditional:</td><td></td></tr>
<tr><td>   Gothic/Tudor</td><td>▲</td></tr>
<tr><td>   Georgian/Colonial</td><td>▲▲</td></tr>
<tr><td>   Victorian</td><td>▲</td></tr>
<tr><td>   French periods</td><td>▲</td></tr>
<tr><td>Modern:</td><td></td></tr>
<tr><td>   Contemporary</td><td>O</td></tr>
<tr><td>   Bauhaus</td><td>O</td></tr>
<tr><td>   Art Deco</td><td>▽</td></tr>
<tr><td>   High Tech</td><td>▽</td></tr>
<tr><td>Mixed styles</td><td>▲</td></tr>
<tr><td colspan="2">ACCESSORIES:</td></tr>
<tr><td>Souvenirs/mementos</td><td>▲▲</td></tr>
<tr><td>Family pictures</td><td>▲▲</td></tr>
<tr><td>Maps and charts</td><td>O</td></tr>
<tr><td>Models (ships, RR, etc.)</td><td>▲</td></tr>
<tr><td>Business charts</td><td>▽</td></tr>
<tr><td>Tackboard/chalk board</td><td>▽</td></tr>
<tr><td>Books and shelves</td><td>▲</td></tr>
<tr><td>Bar</td><td>▲</td></tr>
<tr><td>TV or film projection</td><td>O</td></tr>
<tr><td>Posters</td><td>▲</td></tr>
<tr><td>Photos/advertisements</td><td>▲</td></tr>
<tr><td>Prints (original art)</td><td>▲</td></tr>
<tr><td>Small water color</td><td>▲</td></tr>
<tr><td>Small oil painting</td><td>▲</td></tr>
<tr><td>Major oil painting(s)</td><td>O</td></tr>
<tr><td>Many small art works</td><td>▲</td></tr>
<tr><td>Diplomas or certificates</td><td>▲</td></tr>
<tr><td>Plants</td><td>▲▲</td></tr>
<tr><td>Cut flowers</td><td>▲</td></tr>
</table>

▲▲ *Strongly significant*　▲ *Significant*　O *Neutral*　▽ *Negative significance*　▽▽ *Strongly negative*

Homelike

SIZE:
Large (over 300 sq. ft.)	O
Medium (100-300 sq. ft.)	▲
Small (100 sq. ft. or less)	▽

LOCATION:
Corner	▲
Window-wall	▲
Inside	O

SHAPE:
Square	O
Near-square rectangle	O
Long and narrow	O
Irregular	O
Curved or round	O

LAYOUT:
Symmetrical	O
Non-symmetrical	▲
Irregular	▲▲

WINDOWS:
None	O
One (small)	▲
Two or more	▲
Corner	▲
Glass wall	O
Window to other offices	▽▽

VIEW:
Good to excellent	▲
Indifferent to poor	▽

WINDOW TREATMENT:
Venetian blinds	▲
Vertical louvers	O
Drapery	▲▲

WALLS:
Paint	▲
Vinyl wall covering	O
Fabric or paper	▲
Paneling	▲
Mirror	▽

FLOORS:
Resilient tile or sheet	▽

FLOORS: (continued)
Carpet	▲
Rug or rugs	▲
Hardwood, parquet	▲

CEILING:
Exposed beams/ducts	▽
Acoustical tile	▽
Integrated system	▽▽
Plaster	▲

LIGHTING:
Fluorescent, standard	▽▽
Fluorscent, low-bright	▽▽
Incandescent, recessed	▲
Indirect	O
Lamps	▲▲

FURNITURE:
Desk:	
Large	▽
Small	▲
Closed-front	▽
Open, or table	O
Curved or round	▲▲
No desk (work counter)	▲
Conference table:	
rectangular	O
round	O
Lounge seating:	
2 or 3 chairs	▲
sofa and table group	▲▲

COLORS:
Warm:	
Reds and pinks	▲
Oranges	▲
Yellows	▲
Cool:	
Greens	▲
Blues	▲
Violets and purples	O
Neutral:	
White	▲
Grays	O

COLORS: (continued)
Black	O
Browns	▲
Tans and beiges	▲▲

TEXTURES:
Smooth, slick, shiny	▽
Natural, fuzzy, heavy	▲
Metallics	▽

STYLES:
Traditional:	
Gothic/Tudor	▲
Georgian/Colonial	▲▲
Victorian	▲▲
French periods	▲
Modern:	
Contemporary	▲
Bauhaus	O
Art Deco	O
High Tech	▽
Mixed styles	▲

ACCESSORIES:
Souvenirs/mementos	▲▲
Family pictures	▲▲
Maps and charts	▲
Models (ships, RR, etc.)	▲
Business charts	▽
Tackboard/chalk board	▽
Books and shelves	▲▲
Bar	O
TV or film projection	O
Posters	O
Photos/advertisements	O
Prints (original art)	▲
Small water color	▲
Small oil painting	▲
Major oil painting(s)	O
Many small art works	▲
Diplomas or certificates	▲
Plants	▲▲
Cut flowers	▲

▲▲ *Strongly significant* ▲ *Significant* O *Neutral* ▽ *Negative significance* ▽▽ *Strongly negative*

Active

<table>
<tr><td colspan="2">SIZE:</td></tr>
<tr><td>Large (over 300 sq. ft.)</td><td>O</td></tr>
<tr><td>Medium (100-300 sq. ft.)</td><td>O</td></tr>
<tr><td>Small (100 sq. ft. or less)</td><td>O</td></tr>
<tr><td colspan="2">LOCATION:</td></tr>
<tr><td>Corner</td><td>▲</td></tr>
<tr><td>Window-wall</td><td>▲</td></tr>
<tr><td>Inside</td><td>O</td></tr>
<tr><td colspan="2">SHAPE:</td></tr>
<tr><td>Square</td><td>O</td></tr>
<tr><td>Near-square rectangle</td><td>O</td></tr>
<tr><td>Long and narrow</td><td>O</td></tr>
<tr><td>Irregular</td><td>▲</td></tr>
<tr><td>Curved or round</td><td>▲</td></tr>
<tr><td colspan="2">LAYOUT:</td></tr>
<tr><td>Symmetrical</td><td>O</td></tr>
<tr><td>Non-symmetrical</td><td>▲</td></tr>
<tr><td>Irregular</td><td>▲</td></tr>
<tr><td colspan="2">WINDOWS:</td></tr>
<tr><td>None</td><td>O</td></tr>
<tr><td>One (small)</td><td>O</td></tr>
<tr><td>Two or more</td><td>▲</td></tr>
<tr><td>Corner</td><td>▲</td></tr>
<tr><td>Glass wall</td><td>▲</td></tr>
<tr><td>Window to other offices</td><td>▲</td></tr>
<tr><td colspan="2">VIEW:</td></tr>
<tr><td>Good to excellent</td><td>O</td></tr>
<tr><td>Indifferent to poor</td><td>O</td></tr>
<tr><td colspan="2">WINDOW TREATMENT:</td></tr>
<tr><td>Venetian blinds</td><td>O</td></tr>
<tr><td>Vertical louvers</td><td>▲</td></tr>
<tr><td>Drapery</td><td>▽</td></tr>
<tr><td colspan="2">WALLS:</td></tr>
<tr><td>Paint</td><td>O</td></tr>
<tr><td>Vinyl wall covering</td><td>O</td></tr>
<tr><td>Fabric or paper</td><td>O</td></tr>
<tr><td>Paneling</td><td>O</td></tr>
<tr><td>Mirror</td><td>▲</td></tr>
<tr><td colspan="2">FLOORS:</td></tr>
<tr><td>Resilient tile or sheet</td><td>▲</td></tr>
</table>

<table>
<tr><td colspan="2">FLOORS: (continued)</td></tr>
<tr><td>Carpet</td><td>▲</td></tr>
<tr><td>Rug or rugs</td><td>O</td></tr>
<tr><td>Hardwood, parquet</td><td>O</td></tr>
<tr><td colspan="2">CEILING:</td></tr>
<tr><td>Exposed beams/ducts</td><td>▲</td></tr>
<tr><td>Acoustical tile</td><td>O</td></tr>
<tr><td>Integrated system</td><td>▲</td></tr>
<tr><td>Plaster</td><td>▽</td></tr>
<tr><td colspan="2">LIGHTING:</td></tr>
<tr><td>Fluorescent, standard</td><td>▲</td></tr>
<tr><td>Fluorscent, low-bright</td><td>▽</td></tr>
<tr><td>Incandescent, recessed</td><td>▽</td></tr>
<tr><td>Indirect</td><td>▽▽</td></tr>
<tr><td>Lamps</td><td>▲</td></tr>
<tr><td colspan="2">FURNITURE:</td></tr>
<tr><td>Desk:</td><td></td></tr>
<tr><td>Large</td><td>O</td></tr>
<tr><td>Small</td><td>O</td></tr>
<tr><td>Closed-front</td><td>O</td></tr>
<tr><td>Open, or table</td><td>▲</td></tr>
<tr><td>Curved or round</td><td>O</td></tr>
<tr><td>No desk (work counter)</td><td>▲</td></tr>
<tr><td>Conference table:</td><td></td></tr>
<tr><td>rectangular</td><td>O</td></tr>
<tr><td>round</td><td>▲</td></tr>
<tr><td>Lounge seating:</td><td></td></tr>
<tr><td>2 or 3 chairs</td><td>O</td></tr>
<tr><td>sofa and table group</td><td>O</td></tr>
<tr><td colspan="2">COLORS:</td></tr>
<tr><td>Warm:</td><td></td></tr>
<tr><td>Reds and pinks</td><td>▲</td></tr>
<tr><td>Oranges</td><td>▲</td></tr>
<tr><td>Yellows</td><td>▲</td></tr>
<tr><td>Cool:</td><td></td></tr>
<tr><td>Greens</td><td>O</td></tr>
<tr><td>Blues</td><td>O</td></tr>
<tr><td>Violets and purples</td><td>▲</td></tr>
<tr><td>Neutral:</td><td></td></tr>
<tr><td>White</td><td>▲</td></tr>
<tr><td>Grays</td><td>▽</td></tr>
</table>

<table>
<tr><td colspan="2">COLORS: (continued)</td></tr>
<tr><td>Black</td><td>▽</td></tr>
<tr><td>Browns</td><td>▽</td></tr>
<tr><td>Tans and beiges</td><td>▽</td></tr>
<tr><td colspan="2">TEXTURES:</td></tr>
<tr><td>Smooth, slick, shiny</td><td>▲</td></tr>
<tr><td>Natural, fuzzy, heavy</td><td>O</td></tr>
<tr><td>Metallics</td><td>▲</td></tr>
<tr><td colspan="2">STYLES:</td></tr>
<tr><td>Traditional:</td><td></td></tr>
<tr><td>Gothic/Tudor</td><td>▽▽</td></tr>
<tr><td>Georgian/Colonial</td><td>▽</td></tr>
<tr><td>Victorian</td><td>▽</td></tr>
<tr><td>French periods</td><td>▽▽</td></tr>
<tr><td>Modern:</td><td></td></tr>
<tr><td>Contemporary</td><td>▲</td></tr>
<tr><td>Bauhaus</td><td>▲</td></tr>
<tr><td>Art Deco</td><td>▲</td></tr>
<tr><td>High Tech</td><td>▲▲</td></tr>
<tr><td>Mixed styles</td><td>▲</td></tr>
<tr><td colspan="2">ACCESSORIES:</td></tr>
<tr><td>Souvenirs/mementos</td><td>▲</td></tr>
<tr><td>Family pictures</td><td>▽</td></tr>
<tr><td>Maps and charts</td><td>▲</td></tr>
<tr><td>Models (ships, RR, etc.)</td><td>▲</td></tr>
<tr><td>Business charts</td><td>▲</td></tr>
<tr><td>Tackboard/chalk board</td><td>▲</td></tr>
<tr><td>Books and shelves</td><td>▲</td></tr>
<tr><td>Bar</td><td>O</td></tr>
<tr><td>TV or film projection</td><td>▲</td></tr>
<tr><td>Posters</td><td>▲</td></tr>
<tr><td>Photos/advertisements</td><td>▲</td></tr>
<tr><td>Prints (original art)</td><td>▲</td></tr>
<tr><td>Small water color</td><td>O</td></tr>
<tr><td>Small oil painting</td><td>O</td></tr>
<tr><td>Major oil painting(s)</td><td>▽</td></tr>
<tr><td>Many small art works</td><td>O</td></tr>
<tr><td>Diplomas or certificates</td><td>O</td></tr>
<tr><td>Plants</td><td>▲</td></tr>
<tr><td>Cut flowers</td><td>▲</td></tr>
</table>

▲▲*Strongly significant*　▲*Significant*　O*Neutral*　▽*Negative significance*　▽▽*Strongly negative*

Calm

SIZE:

Large (over 300 sq. ft.)	O
Medium (100-300 sq. ft.)	O
Small (100 sq. ft. or less)	O

LOCATION:

Corner	O
Window-wall	▲
Inside	▲

SHAPE:

Square	▲
Near-square rectangle	▲
Long and narrow	O
Irregular	▽
Curved or round	▽

LAYOUT:

Symmetrical	▲
Non-symmetrical	O
Irregular	▽

WINDOWS:

None	O
One (small)	▲
Two or more	▲
Corner	▲
Glass wall	O
Window to other offices	▽

VIEW:

Good to excellent	O
Indifferent to poor	O

WINDOW TREATMENT:

Venetian blinds	O
Vertical louvers	▲
Drapery	▲

WALLS:

Paint	▲
Vinyl wall covering	O
Fabric or paper	▲
Paneling	▲
Mirror	▽

FLOORS:

Resilient tile or sheet	▽

FLOORS: (continued)

Carpet	▲
Rug or rugs	O
Hardwood, parquet	O

CEILING:

Exposed beams/ducts	▽▽
Acoustical tile	O
Integrated system	▽
Plaster	▲

LIGHTING:

Fluorescent, standard	▽▽
Fluorscent, low-bright	▲
Incandescent, recessed	▲
Indirect	▲
Lamps	▲

FURNITURE:

Desk:	
Large	O
Small	O
Closed-front	▲
Open, or table	O
Curved or round	▽
No desk (work counter)	▲
Conference table:	
rectangular	O
round	O
Lounge seating:	
2 or 3 chairs	O
sofa and table group	▲

COLORS:

Warm:	
Reds and pinks	▲
Oranges	▽
Yellows	O
Cool:	
Greens	▲
Blues	▲▲
Violets and purples	▲
Neutral:	
White	▲
Grays	▲

COLORS: (continued)

Black	O
Browns	▲
Tans and beiges	▲▲

TEXTURES:

Smooth, slick, shiny	▽
Natural, fuzzy, heavy	▲
Metallics	▽

STYLES:

Traditional:	
Gothic/Tudor	▲
Georgian/Colonial	▲
Victorian	O
French periods	O
Modern:	
Contemporary	▲
Bauhaus	O
Art Deco	▽
High Tech	▽▽
Mixed styles	▽

ACCESSORIES:

Souvenirs/mementos	▲
Family pictures	▲▲
Maps and charts	▲
Models (ships, RR, etc.)	▲
Business charts	O
Tackboard/chalk board	O
Books and shelves	▲
Bar	O
TV or film projection	▽
Posters	▲
Photos/advertisements	O
Prints (original art)	▲
Small water color	▲
Small oil painting	▲
Major oil painting(s)	O
Many small art works	▲
Diplomas or certificates	O
Plants	▲▲
Cut flowers	▲▲

▲▲ *Strongly significant* ▲ *Significant* O *Neutral* ▽ *Negative significance* ▽▽ *Strongly negative*

Urban

SIZE:
Large (over 300 sq. ft.)	▲
Medium (100-300 sq. ft.)	O
Small (100 sq. ft. or less)	O

LOCATION:
Corner	▲
Window-wall	▲
Inside	▲

SHAPE:
Square	▲
Near-square rectangle	▲
Long and narrow	O
Irregular	O
Curved or round	O

LAYOUT:
Symmetrical	O
Non-symmetrical	O
Irregular	O

WINDOWS:
None	▲
One (small)	▲
Two or more	▲
Corner	▲
Glass wall	▲
Window to other offices	▲

VIEW:
Good to excellent	O
Indifferent to poor	O

WINDOW TREATMENT:
Venetian blinds	▲
Vertical louvers	▲
Drapery	O

WALLS:
Paint	▲
Vinyl wall covering	▲
Fabric or paper	O
Paneling	▲
Mirror	O

FLOORS:
Resilient tile or sheet	▲

FLOORS: (continued)
Carpet	▲
Rug or rugs	O
Hardwood, parquet	O

CEILING:
Exposed beams/ducts	O
Acoustical tile	▲
Integrated system	▲
Plaster	O

LIGHTING:
Fluorescent, standard	▲
Fluorscent, low-bright	▲
Incandescent, recessed	▲
Indirect	▲
Lamps	▽

FURNITURE:
Desk:	
Large	O
Small	O
Closed-front	O
Open, or table	O
Curved or round	O
No desk (work counter)	O
Conference table:	
rectangular	O
round	O
Lounge seating:	
2 or 3 chairs	▲
sofa and table group	▲

COLORS:
Warm:	
Reds and pinks	O
Oranges	O
Yellows	O
Cool:	
Greens	O
Blues	O
Violets and purples	▲
Neutral:	
White	▲
Grays	▲

COLORS: (continued)
Black	▲
Browns	O
Tans and beiges	▲

TEXTURES:
Smooth, slick, shiny	▲
Natural, fuzzy, heavy	O
Metallics	▲

STYLES:
Traditional:	
Gothic/Tudor	▽
Georgian/Colonial	O
Victorian	O
French periods	O
Modern:	
Contemporary	▲
Bauhaus	▲
Art Deco	▲
High Tech	▲▲
Mixed styles	▲

ACCESSORIES:
Souvenirs/mementos	O
Family pictures	O
Maps and charts	O
Models (ships, RR, etc.)	O
Business charts	▲
Tackboard/chalk board	▲
Books and shelves	▲
Bar	▲
TV or film projection	▲
Posters	▲
Photos/advertisements	▲
Prints (original art)	▲
Small water color	O
Small oil painting	O
Major oil painting(s)	O
Many small art works	O
Diplomas or certificates	▲
Plants	▲
Cut flowers	O

▲▲ *Strongly significant*　▲ *Significant*　O *Neutral*　▽ *Negative significance*　▽▽ *Strongly negative*

Rural

SIZE:
Large (over 300 sq. ft.)	▽
Medium (100-300 sq. ft.)	O
Small (100 sq. ft. or less)	O

LOCATION:
Corner	▲
Window-wall	▲
Inside	O

SHAPE:
Square	O
Near-square rectangle	O
Long and narrow	O
Irregular	O
Curved or round	O

LAYOUT:
Symmetrical	O
Non-symmetrical	▲
Irregular	▲

WINDOWS:
None	▽
One (small)	▲
Two or more	▲
Corner	▲
Glass wall	▲
Window to other offices	▽

VIEW:
Good to excellent	▲
Indifferent to poor	▽

WINDOW TREATMENT:
Venetian blinds	O
Vertical louvers	▽
Drapery	▲

WALLS:
Paint	▲
Vinyl wall covering	O
Fabric or paper	O
Paneling	O
Mirror	▽

FLOORS:
Resilient tile or sheet	▽

FLOORS: (continued)
Carpet	O
Rug or rugs	▲
Hardwood, parquet	▲

CEILING:
Exposed beams/ducts	O
Acoustical tile	O
Integrated system	O
Plaster	▲

LIGHTING:
Fluorescent, standard	▽▽
Fluorscent, low-bright	▽
Incandescent, recessed	O
Indirect	O
Lamps	▲▲

FURNITURE:
Desk:	
Large	O
Small	O
Closed-front	O
Open, or table	O
Curved or round	▽
No desk (work counter)	O
Conference table:	
rectangular	O
round	O
Lounge seating:	
2 or 3 chairs	O
sofa and table group	O

COLORS:
Warm:	
Reds and pinks	O
Oranges	O
Yellows	▲
Cool:	
Greens	▲
Blues	▲
Violets and purples	O
Neutral:	
White	O
Grays	O

COLORS: (continued)
Black	▽
Browns	▲
Tans and beiges	▲

TEXTURES:
Smooth, slick, shiny	▽
Natural, fuzzy, heavy	▲▲
Metallics	▽

STYLES:
Traditional:	
Gothic/Tudor	▽
Georgian/Colonial	▲
Victorian	▲
French periods	▽
Modern:	
Contemporary	▽
Bauhaus	▽
Art Deco	▽
High Tech	▽
Mixed styles	▲

ACCESSORIES:
Souvenirs/mementos	▲
Family pictures	▲
Maps and charts	O
Models (ships, RR, etc.)	O
Business charts	O
Tackboard/chalk board	▲
Books and shelves	▲
Bar	▽
TV or film projection	▽
Posters	O
Photos/advertisements	O
Prints (original art)	O
Small water color	O
Small oil painting	O
Major oil painting(s)	▽
Many small art works	▽
Diplomas or certificates	O
Plants	▲▲
Cut flowers	O

▲▲ *Strongly significant* ▲*Significant* O*Neutral* ▽ *Negative significance* ▽▽*Strongly negative*

Economical

SIZE:

Large (over 300 sq. ft.)	▽▽
Medium (100-300 sq. ft.)	O
Small (100 sq. ft. or less)	▲

LOCATION:

Corner	▽
Window-wall	O
Inside	▲▲

SHAPE:

Square	▲
Near-square rectangle	▲
Long and narrow	O
Irregular	▽
Curved or round	▽

LAYOUT:

Symmetrical	O
Non-symmetrical	O
Irregular	O

WINDOWS:

None	▲
One (small)	▲
Two or more	O
Corner	O
Glass wall	▽
Window to other offices	▲

VIEW:

Good to excellent	▽
Indifferent to poor	O

WINDOW TREATMENT:

Venetian blinds	▲
Vertical louvers	O
Drapery	O

WALLS:

Paint	▲
Vinyl wall covering	O
Fabric or paper	O
Paneling	▽
Mirror	▽▽

FLOORS:

Resilient tile or sheet	▲▲

FLOORS: (continued)

Carpet	O
Rug or rugs	▽
Hardwood, parquet	▽

CEILING:

Exposed beams/ducts	▲▲
Acoustical tile	▲
Integrated system	O
Plaster	O

LIGHTING:

Fluorescent, standard	▲▲
Fluorscent, low-bright	▲
Incandescent, recessed	O
Indirect	▽
Lamps	▽

FURNITURE:

Desk:	
Large	▽
Small	▲
Closed-front	▲
Open, or table	O
Curved or round	▽
No desk (work counter)	▲
Conference table:	
rectangular	▲
round	O
Lounge seating:	
2 or 3 chairs	▲
sofa and table group	O

COLORS:

Warm:	
Reds and pinks	O
Oranges	O
Yellows	▲
Cool:	
Greens	▲
Blues	▲
Violets and purples	O
Neutral:	
White	▲
Grays	O

COLORS: (continued)

Black	O
Browns	▲
Tans and beiges	▲▲

TEXTURES:

Smooth, slick, shiny	▽
Natural, fuzzy, heavy	▲
Metallics	O

STYLES:

Traditional:	
Gothic/Tudor	▽
Georgian/Colonial	▽
Victorian	▽
French periods	▽▽
Modern:	
Contemporary	▲
Bauhaus	▲
Art Deco	▲
High Tech	▲
Mixed styles	▲

ACCESSORIES:

Souvenirs/mementos	O
Family pictures	O
Maps and charts	O
Models (ships, RR, etc.)	O
Business charts	O
Tackboard/chalk board	▲
Books and shelves	O
Bar	O
TV or film projection	O
Posters	▲
Photos/advertisements	▲
Prints (original art)	▲
Small water color	O
Small oil painting	O
Major oil painting(s)	▽
Many small art works	▲
Diplomas or certificates	▲
Plants	▲
Cut flowers	O

▲▲ *Strongly significant*   ▲ *Significant*   O *Neutral*   ▽ *Negative significance*   ▽▽ *Strongly negative*

Luxurious

SIZE:

Large (over 300 sq. ft.)	▲▲
Medium (100-300 sq. ft.)	▲
Small (100 sq. ft. or less)	O

LOCATION:

Corner	▲▲
Window-wall	▲
Inside	O

SHAPE:

Square	O
Near-square rectangle	O
Long and narrow	▽
Irregular	▲
Curved or round	▲▲

LAYOUT:

Symmetrical	▲
Non-symmetrical	▲
Irregular	▲

WINDOWS:

None	▽▽
One (small)	▽
Two or more	O
Corner	▲
Glass wall	▲▲
Window to other offices	▽

VIEW:

Good to excellent	▲▲
Indifferent to poor	▽▽

WINDOW TREATMENT:

Venetian blinds	▽
Vertical louvers	▲
Drapery	▲▲

WALLS:

Paint	O
Vinyl wall covering	▲
Fabric or paper	▲▲
Paneling	▲▲
Mirror	▲▲

FLOORS:

Resilient tile or sheet	▽▽

FLOORS: (continued)

Carpet	O
Rug or rugs	▲▲
Hardwood, parquet	▲

CEILING:

Exposed beams/ducts	▽
Acoustical tile	▽
Integrated system	O
Plaster	▲

LIGHTING:

Fluorescent, standard	▽▽
Fluorscent, low-bright	▲
Incandescent, recessed	▲
Indirect	▲
Lamps	▲

FURNITURE:

Desk:	
Large	▲
Small	▽
Closed-front	O
Open, or table	O
Curved or round	▲
No desk (work counter)	▲
Conference table:	
rectangular	▽
round	▲
Lounge seating:	
2 or 3 chairs	O
sofa and table group	▲

COLORS:

Warm:	
Reds and pinks	O
Oranges	O
Yellows	O
Cool:	
Greens	O
Blues	▲
Violets and purples	▲▲
Neutral:	
White	▲
Grays	▲

COLORS: (continued)

Black	▲
Browns	▲▲
Tans and beiges	▲

TEXTURES:

Smooth, slick, shiny	O
Natural, fuzzy, heavy	▲▲
Metallics	▲

STYLES:

Traditional:	
Gothic/Tudor	▲
Georgian/Colonial	▲▲
Victorian	▲
French periods	▲▲
Modern:	
Contemporary	▲
Bauhaus	▲
Art Deco	▲▲
High Tech	▲
Mixed styles	O

ACCESSORIES:

Souvenirs/mementos	O
Family pictures	O
Maps and charts	O
Models (ships, RR, etc.)	O
Business charts	O
Tackboard/chalk board	▽
Books and shelves	▲
Bar	▲▲
TV or film projection	▲
Posters	▽
Photos/advertisements	▽
Prints (original art)	▽
Small water color	▲
Small oil painting	▲
Major oil painting(s)	▲▲
Many small art works	▲▲
Diplomas or certificates	▽
Plants	▲▲
Cut flowers	▲

▲▲ *Strongly significant*   ▲ *Significant*   O *Neutral*   ▽ *Negative significance*   ▽▽ *Strongly negative*

Modern

SIZE:	
Large (over 300 sq. ft.)	▲
Medium (100-300 sq. ft.)	▲
Small (100 sq. ft. or less)	O

LOCATION:	
Corner	▲
Window-wall	▲
Inside	O

SHAPE:	
Square	O
Near-square rectangle	O
Long and narrow	O
Irregular	▲
Curved or round	▲

LAYOUT:	
Symmetrical	O
Non-symmetrical	▲
Irregular	▲▲

WINDOWS:	
None	O
One (small)	▽
Two or more	▲
Corner	▲▲
Glass wall	▲▲
Window to other offices	▲

VIEW:	
Good to excellent	▲
Indifferent to poor	▽

WINDOW TREATMENT:	
Venetian blinds	▲
Vertical louvers	▲▲
Drapery	▽

WALLS:	
Paint	▲
Vinyl wall covering	▲
Fabric or paper	O
Paneling	O
Mirror	O

FLOORS:	
Resilient tile or sheet	O

FLOORS: (continued)	
Carpet	▲
Rug or rugs	▽
Hardwood, parquet	O

CEILING:	
Exposed beams/ducts	▲
Acoustical tile	O
Integrated system	▲
Plaster	O

LIGHTING:	
Fluorescent, standard	▽
Fluorscent, low-bright	▲
Incandescent, recessed	▲
Indirect	▲
Lamps	▽

FURNITURE:	
Desk:	
Large	O
Small	O
Closed-front	O
Open, or table	▲
Curved or round	▲
No desk (work counter)	▲▲
Conference table:	
rectangular	O
round	▲
Lounge seating:	
2 or 3 chairs	▲
sofa and table group	▲

COLORS:	
Warm:	
Reds and pinks	O
Oranges	O
Yellows	▲
Cool:	
Greens	O
Blues	O
Violets and purples	O
Neutral:	
White	▲▲
Grays	▲

COLORS: (continued)	
Black	▲
Browns	O
Tans and beiges	O

TEXTURES:	
Smooth, slick, shiny	▲
Natural, fuzzy, heavy	▲
Metallics	▲

STYLES:	
Traditional:	
Gothic/Tudor	▽▽
Georgian/Colonial	▽▽
Victorian	▽▽
French periods	▽▽
Modern:	
Contemporary	▲
Bauhaus	▲▲
Art Deco	▲▲
High Tech	▲▲
Mixed styles	▲

ACCESSORIES:	
Souvenirs/mementos	O
Family pictures	O
Maps and charts	▲
Models (ships, RR, etc.)	▲
Business charts	O
Tackboard/chalk board	▲
Books and shelves	▲
Bar	▲
TV or film projection	▲
Posters	▲
Photos/advertisements	▲
Prints (original art)	▲
Small water color	O
Small oil painting	O
Major oil painting(s)	O
Many small art works	O
Diplomas or certificates	O
Plants	▲
Cut flowers	▲

▲▲ *Strongly significant* ▲ *Significant* O *Neutral* ▽ *Negative significance* ▽▽ *Strongly negative*

Traditional

SIZE:	
Large (over 300 sq. ft.)	O
Medium (100-300 sq. ft.)	O
Small (100 sq. ft. or less)	O

LOCATION:	
Corner	▲
Window-wall	▲
Inside	O

SHAPE:	
Square	▲
Near-square rectangle	▲
Long and narrow	O
Irregular	▽
Curved or round	▽▽

LAYOUT:	
Symmetrical	▲▲
Non-symmetrical	O
Irregular	▽

WINDOWS:	
None	O
One (small)	▲
Two or more	▲
Corner	▲
Glass wall	▽
Window to other offices	▽▽

VIEW:	
Good to excellent	O
Indifferent to poor	O

WINDOW TREATMENT:	
Venetian blinds	▲
Vertical louvers	▽
Drapery	▲▲

WALLS:	
Paint	O
Vinyl wall covering	O
Fabric or paper	▲
Paneling	▲▲
Mirror	▽

FLOORS:	
Resilient tile or sheet	▽

FLOORS: (continued)	
Carpet	O
Rug or rugs	▲
Hardwood, parquet	▲

CEILING:	
Exposed beams/ducts	▽
Acoustical tile	▽
Integrated system	▽▽
Plaster	▲

LIGHTING:	
Fluorescent, standard	▽▽
Fluorscent, low-bright	O
Incandescent, recessed	▲
Indirect	▲
Lamps	▲▲

FURNITURE:	
Desk:	
Large	O
Small	O
Closed-front	▲
Open, or table	▽
Curved or round	▽
No desk (work counter)	▽
Conference table:	
rectangular	O
round	O
Lounge seating:	
2 or 3 chairs	O
sofa and table group	O

COLORS:	
Warm:	
Reds and pinks	O
Oranges	▽
Yellows	O
Cool:	
Greens	▲
Blues	▲
Violets and purples	▽
Neutral:	
White	O
Grays	O

COLORS: (continued)	
Black	▽
Browns	▲
Tans and beiges	▲

TEXTURES:	
Smooth, slick, shiny	▽▽
Natural, fuzzy, heavy	▲
Metallics	▽

STYLES:	
Traditional:	
Gothic/Tudor	▲
Georgian/Colonial	▲
Victorian	▲
French periods	▲
Modern:	
Contemporary	▽
Bauhaus	▽▽
Art Deco	▽▽
High Tech	▽▽
Mixed styles	▽

ACCESSORIES:	
Souvenirs/mementos	▲
Family pictures	▲
Maps and charts	▲
Models (ships, RR, etc.)	O
Business charts	O
Tackboard/chalk board	▽
Books and shelves	▲
Bar	O
TV or film projection	▽
Posters	▽
Photos/advertisements	▽
Prints (original art)	O
Small water color	▲
Small oil painting	▲
Major oil painting(s)	▲
Many small art works	▲
Diplomas or certificates	▲
Plants	▲
Cut flowers	▲

▲▲ *Strongly significant*   ▲ *Significant*   O *Neutral*   ▽ *Negative significance*   ▽▽ *Strongly negative*

Conservative

SIZE:	
Large (over 300 sq. ft.)	O
Medium (100-300 sq. ft.)	▲▲
Small (100 sq. ft. or less)	O

LOCATION:	
Corner	▲
Window-wall	▲
Inside	O

SHAPE:	
Square	▲
Near-square rectangle	▲
Long and narrow	O
Irregular	▽▽
Curved or round	▽▽

LAYOUT:	
Symmetrical	▲▲
Non-symmetrical	O
Irregular	▽

WINDOWS:	
None	O
One (small)	▲
Two or more	▲
Corner	▲
Glass wall	▽▽
Window to other offices	▽▽

VIEW:	
Good to excellent	O
Indifferent to poor	O

WINDOW TREATMENT:	
Venetian blinds	▲
Vertical louvers	▽
Drapery	▲▲

WALLS:	
Paint	O
Vinyl wall covering	O
Fabric or paper	▲
Paneling	▲▲
Mirror	▽

FLOORS:	
Resilient tile or sheet	O

FLOORS: (continued)	
Carpet	▲
Rug or rugs	▲
Hardwood, parquet	▲

CEILING:	
Exposed beams/ducts	▽
Acoustical tile	O
Integrated system	▽
Plaster	▲

LIGHTING:	
Fluorescent, standard	▽▽
Fluorscent, low-bright	▲
Incandescent, recessed	▲
Indirect	O
Lamps	▲

FURNITURE:	
Desk:	
Large	O
Small	O
Closed-front	▲
Open, or table	▽▽
Curved or round	▽
No desk (work counter)	▽▽
Conference table:	
rectangular	O
round	▽
Lounge seating:	
2 or 3 chairs	O
sofa and table group	O

COLORS:	
Warm:	
Reds and pinks	O
Oranges	▽
Yellows	O
Cool:	
Greens	▲
Blues	▲
Violets and purples	▽
Neutral:	
White	O
Grays	O

COLORS: (continued)	
Black	▽
Browns	▲▲
Tans and beiges	▲▲

TEXTURES:	
Smooth, slick, shiny	▽
Natural, fuzzy, heavy	▲
Metallics	▽

STYLES:	
Traditional:	
Gothic/Tudor	▲
Georgian/Colonial	▲▲
Victorian	▲
French periods	▲▲
Modern:	
Contemporary	▽
Bauhaus	▽▽
Art Deco	▽
High Tech	▽▽
Mixed styles	O

ACCESSORIES:	
Souvenirs/mementos	▲
Family pictures	▲
Maps and charts	O
Models (ships, RR, etc.)	O
Business charts	▽
Tackboard/chalk board	▽▽
Books and shelves	▲
Bar	▽
TV or film projection	▽
Posters	▽▽
Photos/advertisements	▽▽
Prints (original art)	▽
Small water color	▲
Small oil painting	▲
Major oil painting(s)	▲
Many small art works	▲
Diplomas or certificates	▲
Plants	▲
Cut flowers	▲

▲▲ *Strongly significant*   ▲ *Significant*   O *Neutral*   ▽ *Negative significance*   ▽▽ *Strongly negative*

High-style

SIZE:	
Large (over 300 sq. ft.)	O
Medium (100-300 sq. ft.)	O
Small (100 sq. ft. or less)	O

LOCATION:	
Corner	▲
Window-wall	▲
Inside	▽

SHAPE:	
Square	O
Near-square rectangle	O
Long and narrow	▽
Irregular	▲
Curved or round	▲

LAYOUT:	
Symmetrical	O
Non-symmetrical	▲
Irregular	▲

WINDOWS:	
None	▽
One (small)	▽
Two or more	▲
Corner	▲
Glass wall	▲▲
Window to other offices	▽

VIEW:	
Good to excellent	O
Indifferent to poor	O

WINDOW TREATMENT:	
Venetian blinds	O
Vertical louvers	▲
Drapery	O

WALLS:	
Paint	O
Vinyl wall covering	O
Fabric or paper	O
Paneling	O
Mirror	▲

FLOORS:	
Resilient tile or sheet	O

FLOORS: (continued)	
Carpet	▲
Rug or rugs	O
Hardwood, parquet	O

CEILING:	
Exposed beams/ducts	▲
Acoustical tile	O
Integrated system	▲
Plaster	▽

LIGHTING:	
Fluorescent, standard	▽
Fluorscent, low-bright	▲
Incandescent, recessed	▲
Indirect	▲
Lamps	▲

FURNITURE:	
Desk:	
Large	O
Small	O
Closed-front	▽
Open, or table	▲
Curved or round	▲
No desk (work counter)	▲
Conference table:	
rectangular	O
round	▲
Lounge seating:	
2 or 3 chairs	▲
sofa and table group	▲

COLORS:	
Warm:	
Reds and pinks	O
Oranges	O
Yellows	▲
Cool:	
Greens	▽
Blues	▽
Violets and purples	▲
Neutral:	
White	▲▲
Grays	O

COLORS: (continued)	
Black	▲
Browns	O
Tans and beiges	O

TEXTURES:	
Smooth, slick, shiny	▲
Natural, fuzzy, heavy	O
Metallics	▲

STYLES:	
Traditional:	
Gothic/Tudor	▽▽
Georgian/Colonial	▽
Victorian	O
French periods	▽
Modern:	
Contemporary	▲
Bauhaus	▲▲
Art Deco	▲▲
High Tech	▲▲
Mixed styles	▲

ACCESSORIES:	
Souvenirs/mementos	O
Family pictures	▽
Maps and charts	▽
Models (ships, RR, etc.)	▽
Business charts	▽
Tackboard/chalk board	▽
Books and shelves	O
Bar	▲
TV or film projection	▲
Posters	▲
Photos/advertisements	▲
Prints (original art)	O
Small water color	▽
Small oil painting	▽
Major oil painting(s)	▲
Many small art works	O
Diplomas or certificates	▽
Plants	▲
Cut flowers	▲

▲▲ *Strongly significant* ▲*Significant* O*Neutral* ▽*Negative significance* ▽▽*Strongly negative*

Manufacturers And Distributors

All-Steel Equipment
437 Madison Ave.
New York, NY   10022

Armstrong Cork Company
Liberty & Charlotte Sts.
Lancaster, PA   17604

Atelier International, Inc.
595 Madison Ave.
New York, NY   10022

Baker Furniture
Exhibitors Building
Grand Rapids, MI   49503

Brickel Associates Inc.
515 Madison Ave.
New York, NY   10022

L.E. Carpenter and Co.
170 N. Main St.
Wharton, NJ   07885

Castelli Furniture, Inc.
950 Third Ave.
New York, NY   10022

Couristan
919 Third Ave.
New York, NY   10022

Edward Fields
232 E. 59th St.
New York, NY   10022

Eldon Office Products
5330 W. 102 St.
Los Angeles, CA   90045

Forms & Surfaces
Box 5215
Santa Barbara, CA   93108

Glassform Architectural Products
1435 S. Sante Fe Ave.
Compton, CA   90221

GF Business Equipment, Inc.
200 Park Ave.
New York, NY   10017

Heuga USA, Inc.
185 Summer Ave.
Kenilworth, NJ   07033

ICF
145 E. 57th St.
New York, NY   10022

JG Furniture Co.
Quakertown, PA   18951

Kittinger
1893 Elmwood Avenue
Buffalo, NY   14207

Knoll International
745 Fifth Ave.
New York, NY   10022

George Kovacs Lighting, Inc.
831 Madison Avenue
New York, NY   10021

Boris Kroll Fabrics, Inc.
979 Third Ave.
New York, NY   10022

Jack Lenor Larsen, Inc.
232 E. 59th St.
New York, NY   10022

Levalor Lorentzen, Inc.
720 Monroe St.
Hoboken, NJ   07030

Lightolier, Inc.
346 Claremont Ave.
Jersey City, NJ   07305

Herman Miller, Inc.
Zeeland, MI   49464

Myrtle Desk Co.
150 E. 58th St.
New York, NY   10022

Oxford Pendaflex Corp.
Clinton Rd.
Garden City, NY   11530

Peter Pepper Products
17929 S. Susana Rd.
Compton, CA   90221

Harvey Probber Associates
979 Third Ave.
New York, NY   10022

Richard Racana Jr. & Assoc.
Planum Inc. System
1218 Merchandise Mart
Chicago, IL   60654

Scalamandre Silks, Inc.
950 Third Ave.
New York, NY   10022

Schumacher
919 Third Ave.
New York, NY   10022

Isabel Scott Fabrics
979 Third Ave.
New York, NY   10022

Shaw-Walker Company
45 Division Street
Muskegon, MI   49443

Steelcase, Inc.
Grand Rapids, MI   49508

Stendig, Inc.
410 E. 62nd St.
New York, NY   10021

Supreme Equipment and Systems Corp.
170 53rd St.
Brooklyn, NY   11232

Thailand Teakwood Importers, Inc.
645 N. Michigan Avenue
Chicago, IL   60611

Thayer Coggin Institutional, Inc.
South Road
High Point, NC   27262

Thonet Industries, Inc.
491 E. Prince St.
York, PA   17405

Zographos Designs
150 E. 58th St.
New York, NY   10022

Further Reading

The books dealing with office design and planning are surprisingly few in number. The following list includes those most current and most widely available.

Duffy, F., Cave, C., and Worthington, J. et al., *Planning Office Space.,* Architectural Press, London, and Nichols Publishing, New York, 1976. A very thorough treatise written from a characteristically British point of view.

Friedmann, A., Pile, J. and Wilson, F. *Interior Design: An Introduction to Architectural Interiors;* 2nd Ed., Elsevier North Holland, New York, 1976; Japanese edition, Shokokusha, 1973. A general text on interior design, but with coverage of most aspects of office design.

Illuminating Engineering Society Lighting Handbook; I.E.S., New York, 1959 and later editions. Highly technical, but the definitive reference on this subject.

Pile, John F., *Interiors Third Book of Offices,* Whitney Library of Design, New York, 1976.

Pile, John F., *Open Office Planning,* Whitney Library of Design, New York, 1978. Primarily concerned with "open" or "landscape" office planning.

Propst, R. and Wodka, M., *Action Office Acoustics Handbook,* Herman Miller, Inc., Zeeland, Mich., 1975

Propst, R., *The Office: A Facility Based on Change,* Business Press, New York, 1968; also available from Herman Miller, Inc., Zeeland, Mich.

Saphier, Michael, *Office Planning and Design,* McGraw-Hill, New York, 1968; 2nd edition, 1978.

Schmertz,M.F., editor, *Office Building Design,*Architectural Record Books, New York, 1978.

Shoshkes, Lila, *Space Planning,* Architectural Record Books New York 1967.

Steele and Jenks, *The Feel of the Workplace,* Addison-Wesley Publishing Co., 1977.

In addition to books, a good source of material on office planning are the periodicals addressed to the professions of architecture, interior design, and office design. The best-known magazines that carry frequent articles on office design are listed below. They are usually available in larger libraries. Bound volumes from the past few years contain reports on office projects and articles dealing with various details of design and construction. All are monthlies.

Architectural Record, McGraw-Hill, New York.
Contract, Gralia Publications, New York.
Interior Design, Whitney Communications, New York.
Interiors, Billboard Publications, New York.
Progressive Architecture, Reinhold Publishing, Greenwich, Conn.

Index